T0269756

LEARNED EXCELLENCE

Also by Alan Eagle

How Google Works
(with Eric Schmidt and
Jonathan Rosenberg)

Trillion Dollar Coach:
The Leadership Playbook of Silicon
Valley's Bill Campbell
(with Eric Schmidt and
Jonathan Rosenberg)

LEARNED EXCELLENCE

MENTAL DISCIPLINES FOR
LEADING AND WINNING
FROM THE WORLD'S TOP
PERFORMERS

ERIC POTTERAT, PhD,
AND ALAN EAGLE

HARPER
BUSINESS

An Imprint of HarperCollins*Publishers*

HarperCollins books may be purchased for educational, business, or sales promotional use. For information, please email the Special Markets Department at SPsales@harpercollins.com.

FIRST EDITION

Designed by Michele Cameron

Library of Congress Cataloging-in-Publication Data has been applied for.

ISBN 978-0-06-331616-4

24 25 26 27 28 LBC 7 6 5 4 3

To Andrea, Lauren, Bryce,
Tamara, Will, Andie, Nolan, and Claire,
who inspire us to learn excellence every day

CONTENTS

LEARNED
EXCELLENCE

CHAPTER 1

You the Performer

You are a Navy SEAL, in the helicopter en route to a mission. You check and recheck your equipment; everything is sound and ready to go. You look around at your teammates: they are quiet, breathing deeply amid the ruckus of the flight, visualizing what is about to happen. You do the same, closing your eyes and imagining the environment where you will soon find yourself, not just seeing it but feeling, smelling, and hearing it. You review the scenarios you will encounter if everything goes according to plan (like that's gonna happen), and the contingencies if it doesn't. You breathe deeply, intently. The helicopter lands, the door opens.

You are an aerobatic pilot, flying your custom-designed biplane into competition, where you will execute a wide variety of maneuvers that will wow the crowds (and hopefully judges) and subject your body to g-forces that would render just about every other human unconscious. You have your sequence card taped to the instrument panel in front of you, but it is superfluous; you have visualized your routine so many times you almost feel like you have already completed it perfectly. You finish one trick and initiate the next when suddenly you can't see anything. Smoke fills the cockpit. As you lift the canopy to clear the air so you can see again, you feel something warm on your leg. You are flying at 150 mph a thousand feet above the ground, and oil is leaking from the engine.

You are the chief of police of a US city. You have been on the force over thirty years, working your way up from a young cop walking the beat to the leader of a large, diverse force and the voice of public safety in your community. But today you are none of those things. An officer has died in the line of duty, and you are on your way to meet the family. You pull over a few blocks from the home to breathe and center yourself. What happens next is not about you, the police department, or the city. What you say and how you act will help the family start to heal, or not.

You are a US congressman, having served in Washington, DC, for several terms. By now you are getting used to it: the relentless polls telling you if you are liked or not, the never-ending fundraising, the constant planning for the next election. You have authored a bill of which you are very proud. It will make a difference in people's lives, and it may even save some of them. But today it is getting debated on the floor of Congress and the outcome is uncertain. The chairman of the committee is against the bill for various political reasons, so this debate and the subsequent process of marking up your bill are sure to be brutal. You reach into your briefcase, pull out photos of people who will be helped by the bill, and lay them on the table in front of you. This battle is about them, not you. The questions begin.

You are a student walking into a final. It is 50 percent of your grade, in a course that could make or break your chances to get the job you want or get into the college you wish to attend.

You are a parent. Your oldest is suffering the emotional travails of high school social cliques and academic pressures, your youngest is in their room worrying about an upcoming test, and you have a dinner to make and a full email inbox that can't wait until tomorrow.

You are a businessperson, about to make a presentation to a client, partner, or boss. It's about a project that you have been working on for the past six months and care about deeply. You have thirty minutes to convince a skeptical audience that it matters.

You are standing at a podium, about to give a speech. You have your notes in front of you and have practiced a dozen times, but now a live audience fills the room and lights shine in your face. What in the world ever made you think this was a good idea?

You are at a café, waiting for a date. You are excited about this one; you talked over the phone and even FaceTimed for a few minutes, and they made you laugh! You're sipping wine, condensation forms on the glass, they are late. How long will you wait? Then the door swings open and the person whom you have only seen on your phone screen rushes in.

As you read these scenarios you probably can relate more to the last few than the first ones. You are much more likely to be a student, parent, businessperson, reluctant public speaker, or romantic than a Navy SEAL, aerobatics pilot, police officer, or member of the US Congress! But in fact, all of these scenarios have something in common: they are about performance. They describe a situation where a person is about to undertake something challenging where the outcome matters. That challenging thing could be something extreme—surfing a gigantic wave, rushing into a burning building—or it could be something much more mundane—the sales presentation, the science test, the school play. The stakes and degree of difficulty may vary substantially, but the essence does not.

We are all performers. We all regularly undertake challenging things that matter to us. And we all, for the most part, try to do our very best. A few of us are the best at what we do; a lot of us are good and would like to get better. Maybe we're not going to be world champions, but we each have potential and we want to live up to it. So we learn skills, we practice, we read and train, we fail, we chastise ourselves, we suck it up, we practice more, we try again, all in an ongoing effort to get better.

Unfortunately, amid all this training and preparation we tend to ignore the most important component of high performance: the mental aspect. We train everything but our minds. And when the moment arrives, that's what often betrays us.

HARDWARE AND SOFTWARE

In the pages ahead, I'm going to show you how to mentally prepare for and perform in those moments, whether they are big or small, anticipated or spontaneous. My insights, principles, and exercises derive from the work I've been doing for more than three decades. I've developed and managed mental performance programs for the US Navy SEALs, Los Angeles Dodgers, and Red Bull athletes, and worked as a performance coach for leaders from the realms of sports, military, first responders, and business. You could say

I'm a mental performance geek. I love to learn about what makes performers tick, and help them tick better.

All of these experiences and work have brought me face-to-face with thousands of top performers across a range of fields, from military warriors and athletes to businesspeople and first responders. Along the way, I have developed a strong point of view about what separates the very best from the rest. To understand my thesis it helps to look at your phone, that amazing device that likely sits within your reach at this very moment.

Your phone (or tablet or computer) is a great piece of hardware. It's got spiffy processors featuring specifications with words like *bits*, *cores*, and *clock rate*, the latter measured in something called GHz. It has loads of memory, measured in GBs. It has cameras with megapixels, frame rates, and aperture ranges. These are all impressive—they must be, because the ads and reviews tell us they are. They are also useless. To operate, the hardware needs software. Who cares how many GHzs and GBs your phone has? What you care about is getting your messages, watching your videos, posting stuff, playing games, or actually talking to people. The hardware is important, but the operating system and applications are what make the phone perform. You can have the best hardware, but that doesn't matter unless the software keeps up. Software makes everything work!

When I talk to the best performers, the story is always the same. They have great hardware. They are all superb physical and intellectual beings, with skills honed through lots of hard work and repetition, but so are a lot of other people. It is the top performers' mental approach to their craft that sets them apart. They are mentally tough. They don't hold themselves back. They don't worry about what might go wrong and how it will look; they act based on their identity and values, not on what might happen to their reputation. In the moment of stress, they remain calm and cool.

When you watch the very best perform, you think these people are just different. That calmness and confidence, that's innate, right? They must have been born with it!

Nope! They have *learned* how to be excellent. Yes, they may have physical or intellectual traits that set them apart from the rest of us, but even the best are mentally fallible. The champion on the verge of an important competition still perseverates on what could go wrong rather than remembering their great skills and ability. (A text received from one of my clients a few hours before a competition: I find myself doubting myself, any suggestions?) It is what goes on above the neck and between the ears that makes them the very best. The difference between settling and achieving, between good and great, between contentment and fulfillment, is entirely mental. The difference maker, just like in your phone, is the software.

LEARNING EXCELLENCE

Throughout my decades of work with performers, a few common truths have emerged. Just about everyone wants to perform to their very best. We all try to reach our full potential, and maybe a bit more, in every aspect of our lives. Some people are more driven than others, of course. They will work harder and longer, getting the most out of every hour of the day, while the rest of us are fine whiling away an evening watching a show or a game. But the essential human nature is unchanged. We want to be good at what we do in every aspect of our lives. That's part of what makes us happy.[1]

However, most of us sabotage ourselves when it comes to reaching our full potential. Rather than focus on who we are, what we want to achieve, and how we are going to get there, we invest energy in thinking about what might go wrong. What will other people think? What if we fail? How will that look? We act based on reputation rather than identity. We stop taking risks. We worry about failure. We get scared. When we are old and look back on our lives, most of the things we regret are the things we didn't do, not the things we did.[2] Yet we spend a great deal of our time and energy talking ourselves out of doing. I can't do that, I might fail. I can't do that, I'm not very good at it. I can't do that, I'll look bad.

Then, when the moment of performance arrives, we find ourselves at the mercy of our own atavistic fight, flight, or freeze mechanism. Our breathing and heart rates go up, we get butterflies in our stomach, we sweat more, our thoughts race. These reactions may have been helpful back when we were being chased by predators, but in most of today's performance scenarios they are detrimental. We aren't ready for the stress and don't know how to handle it. As a result, we don't achieve our fullest potential.

Don't feel bad; this isn't our fault. For most of history, performance education in any field was primarily hardware-based: strength, endurance, techniques, nutrition, knowledge, and skill. Mental training is traditionally limited to rote learning: how to do something, whether baking a cake or solving an equation. Think back to when you were in school and you had an important test coming up (or back to last week, if you're a student!). Your teacher taught you the material, gave you homework, and maybe told you what stuff would be on the test. But did they teach you how to approach the test? How you could prepare for the pressure of taking it, and how you could calm and refocus yourself when you start to freak out after realizing you're halfway through the period but only a third of the way through the test? Of course not. You were left to learn that for yourself. The hardware was prepped, the software ignored.

This is where performance psychology comes in. It is, at its essence, the process of assessing where the performer is mentally strong and where they need to improve, then learning and practicing mental routines to get better and stronger. I help performers evolve their software so they can get stronger, more resilient, and more confident above the neck and between the ears.

In this book, I distill everything I have learned in my career into a clear set of principles and practices that anyone can use to learn excellence. It is a practical guide to improving your software, so that you can reach your full potential in every aspect of life. Together, we'll learn about five disciplines to learning excellence—think of these as the components of your performance operating system. We start with Values and Goals. What are the things you care about the most? Why do you do what you do? What big, ambitious goals do you want to set for yourself?

Next, we cover Mindset. Maybe you've heard of things like positive mindset and growth mindset, which sound cool, but what do they mean and how do you get there?

After that, Process, as in trust the process and don't worry about the outcome. Which again sounds cool, but . . . what? How can you not worry about the outcome?

Up next, Adversity Tolerance. We are wired to fight, flee, or freeze when confronted with a stressful situation, but that instinct, which helped our species survive eons ago, doesn't work so well in most situations today. What can you do about that?

Then, Balance and Recovery. You are not what you do. There are many different aspects of your life that deserve your attention, but sometimes when you're juggling a bunch of balls you may drop one or two. Some stuff has to wait. Is that OK?

For each of these components, I talk about the practices top performers employ, why they matter, and how they work. I show you how to integrate them into your life, and how you can use them to become a better performer. I illustrate my principles and practices with stories from some of the amazing people with whom I have worked from the military, sports, first responder, and business worlds. I might get a bit nerdy highlighting research that confirms my observations and experiences. I follow each chapter with a Learned Excellence Action Plan, a concise summary of the principles covered in that chapter.

I conclude with a discussion about practicing excellence. How can you put all of these principles into action? Where do you start on day one? How can you overcome the inevitable doubts and obstacles that might get in your way? What can you do to translate the disciplines of Learned Excellence to teammates and colleagues? And—this is a question I get a lot—to your children?

This book distills my experience of working with thousands of performers and interviewing thousands more into an accessible guide and framework that covers all aspects of mental performance—Values and Goals, Mindset, Process, Adversity Tolerance, Balance and Recovery—and gives you clear ideas for how you can practice each one of them. Maybe you aren't a Navy SEAL, a world champion athlete, a first responder, or a business, medical, or political leader. Maybe you're not heading for a nighttime raid where hostiles lurk, or paddling out to surf a giant wave. Maybe you're just a normal person like the rest of us, trying to do well at your job and make good things happen in the world while being a good partner, parent, child, sibling, and friend and having a measure of fun and joy along the way. These things matter, too; in fact they matter the most. They are why you are a performer, and why you want to learn excellence.

Before we get started, let me tell you a bit more about the journey that led me to write this book, and why you can count on me as your guide.

CHAPTER 2

Learning About Excellence

In 1996, after completing the academic portion of my PhD in clinical psychology, I had several internship options. A professor recommended the US Navy, and when I attended one of their open houses I was blown away by the depth and breadth of the experience they offered. My paternal grandfather had served in the Swiss Army during World War II before immigrating to the US with his family in 1956, and I had grown up hearing tales of his war experiences, which included shooting down a German plane from the ground. (Switzerland maintained "armed neutrality" during the war. It did not ally itself with either side and mobilized its military only to defend against invasion. While Germany never invaded, its planes often strayed across the Swiss border. At least one of them didn't make it back.)

My grandparents and their family gave up a lot when they came to the US, arriving here with next to nothing. Everything we had, I gradually came to realize growing up, was due to the risk they had taken and this wonderful country that was now our home. When the opportunity came to serve as a naval officer, I felt it was the least I could do to honor my grandfather's service and my parents' sacrifice, help pay back my family's debt of gratitude to our country, and serve something bigger than myself. Plus, the job was in San Diego, a city my wife, Andrea, and I had come to love while I was doing my PhD work there.

After I successfully completed Officer Indoctrination School (OIS) in 1996, I entered the Navy as a lieutenant and spent the next four years working as a clinical psychologist at the Naval Medical Center in San Diego. My job included providing outpatient individual and group psychotherapy to active-duty Navy personnel; applying psychotherapeutic treatment for anxiety disorders, depressive and adjustment disorders, post-traumatic stress disorder (PTSD), and substance abuse and dependence; evaluating individuals for "fitness for duty" (were they mentally fit for a specialized role?) and security clearance (for example, submarine and weapons screening); performing critical incident debriefing, psycho-diagnostic assessments (personality testing), and "emergency watch" (assessing and helping suicidal or homicidal service members); and teaching. Like I said, the depth and breadth of experience was fantastic.

A few months before my assignment was up, I received an offer to continue my clinical work at the US naval hospital in Rota, Spain. I was coming up on four years of service, so I could have left the Navy and returned to civilian life. Andrea and I went out to dinner one night to talk it over. We had a one-year-old daughter, and it would have been an easy decision to stay put in the comfortable San Diego life we were building. But Andrea brought up a question: Do we want to spend our lives busting our tails in our careers just so we can travel when we retire? Or do we want to see the world now? When she put it that way, there was no doubt that going to Spain was the right answer.

My clinical work continued while at Rota, and I also got to take on the very cool job of working with NASA on space shuttle missions, serving as the "medical regulator" covering the two trans-atlantic landing sites. After the shuttle launched, there was a four-minute window where the mission could be aborted, whereupon the shuttle would be redirected to land at sites in either Morocco or Spain. If such a thing were to happen, it was my job to help the as-tronauts and to serve as an officer on the ground with responsibility for securing the sanctity of the mission and arranging any necessary medical care at non-US facilities. Fortunately, none of the missions I covered were forced to abort, but in my role I got to know and work with several NASA astronauts and leaders.

As my three-year stint in Rota neared its end, I wanted to take my family back home to California. I had fulfilled my obligation to the Navy and could have returned to civilian life, but midway through my Rota tour, on September 11, 2001, the US was attacked. There was no way I was going to resign my commission at that point; serv-ing felt more important than ever. I remembered my grandfather, defending the Swiss border during World War II. Fortunately there was a perfect job available that would put my skills and experience to work: lead psychologist at the Navy SERE school.

THE HIGHEST LEVEL OF STRESS

SERE stands for survival, evasion, resistance, and escape. If you are part of the military and are heading to a posting where you might be in harm's way, SERE school provides you with some very important skills that might come in handy: how to navigate, create shelter, and find food in the wilderness so you can avoid capture, and, if you are captured, how to withstand captivity, sleep deprivation, and other extreme experiences so you can survive and get back home.

SERE entails more than just physical skills training. Evading or experiencing capture exposes a person to levels of stress that most of us can only imagine. People in such a situation live in a near-constant state of "flight, fight, or freeze," which inhibits their ability to think clearly and act effectively. The objective of SERE training is to inoculate its students against that stress by giving them a taste of the challenges they might face if they are caught behind enemy lines. That way, if they ever find themselves in such a scenario, they have more confidence they can get through it.

SERE students are brought to a remote wilderness and trained in survival techniques, then, at an unexpected moment, they are "captured" by authentic-looking bad guys who work for the US military but in their uniforms, language, weapons, and vehicles appear and act very much like enemies. The students are then subjected to an array of experiences that are very close to what they might go through in a real-life prisoner scenario. To say that SERE training is intense is an understatement: its students experience the highest level of stress, as measured by cortisol levels, ever seen in research. At no point are the students in any danger, but that is very hard to remember when you are literally the most stressed-out person on the planet!

When most people start a new job they go through some form of training, and when I took on the SERE role I was no different.

But this was no ordinary orientation. Even though I wasn't going to be shipped out to some dangerous locale, I was headed to the exact same training program I would later be overseeing.

I joined my cohort at a remote, mountainous location, where we trained for a couple of days in navigation and wilderness survival skills. We learned how to evade capture, but not well enough: one day, while we were out running an exercise, we found ourselves suddenly surrounded by several imposing members of an unidentifiable military force ostensibly unfriendly to the United States. They were very authentic-looking baddies, down to their foreign-looking uniforms, foreign-sounding language (I never did figure out what it was), and the non-American vehicles they brought screeching to a halt all around us.

The next several days were some of the most intense of my life. Subjected to interrogation, sleep deprivation, and other unpleasantness, I fought off hallucinations by trying to hang on to the thought that I wasn't actually in danger and by remembering studies I had read of POWs in Vietnam who survived by staying positive and retaining a sense of humor about the situation. By the time I returned home to San Diego, I had gained a newfound appreciation for the rigor of SERE training and lost fifteen pounds.

My new job entailed overseeing the psychological components of the SERE school program, designing new curricula to train students on how to manage extreme stress and scenarios to trigger that stress, all while keeping them safe. This work, which I began in 2003, started my transition from working primarily as a clinical psychologist, helping people overcome mental challenges so they can heal and get back to "normal," to working as a performance psychologist, helping people up their game mentally so they can achieve their highest potential.

(SERE training is somewhat similar to the famous 1971 Stanford Prison Experiment, run by Dr. Philip Zimbardo. During the experiment, Dr. Zimbardo's team created a simulated prison on the Stanford University campus and randomly split up a team of volunteer students into prisoners and guards. The experiment was stopped after only six days (planned duration was two weeks) because some of the guards had started to treat the prisoners sadistically. It was part of my job to ensure nothing similar happened at SERE. I ended up having the honor of sharing some of our work with Dr. Zimbardo.)

At the time, performance psychology was just coming into its own as a branch of the psychology field, so my timing was propitious. A primary component of performance is managing stress, using your mind to control your body at the precise moment when all it wants to do is throw a punch, run away, or curl up in a ball. In my work at SERE, I got to be at the epicenter of the premier stress response training center in the world. I saw firsthand the mental tactics the best performers use to succeed, and what failure mode looks like.

While at SERE I received a top-secret security clearance, which enabled me to work directly with people preparing for or coming back from secret missions. This came in handy when, in addition to my responsibilities at SERE, I was asked to be a lead psychologist on the Navy's repatriation team, working with military personnel who had been detained in other countries and then returned to the US. In this role, I looked out for the person's health and safety, took part in the intelligence debrief, and helped them reintegrate with their family and friends when they got home.

For example, in 2005 I had the incredible task of being the lead psychologist helping Navy SEAL Marcus Luttrell come home. Marcus had survived a battle in Afghanistan that cost the rest of his team their lives. An Afghan village sheltered him for several days until he was rescued. I met Marcus at a base in San Antonio, Texas, as he returned to the States from a base in Germany, and then spent a week with him and his family at their home in Texas, helping him gradually repatriate. Marcus subsequently wrote a book about his experiences, *Lone Survivor*, which later became a movie.

My work with Marcus and others who had been captured showed me just how resilient human beings can be under extreme pressure. There is a wide variety in the backgrounds of people who are captured. Some of them, like SEALs or SERE alumni, are well trained, but others, like truck drivers, may not be. Yet many of the untrained individuals navigate their capture quite well. What gets them through? Positivity and purpose. They want to see their family, kids, and loved ones again. There's no giving up because they have a lot to live for. The power of this motivation, for many, is existential.

SEALS, RED BULL, DODGERS, AND WORLD CUP

In early 2006, Navy Admiral Joseph Maguire, the commander of Naval Special Warfare Command, called me with a new offer. Would I be interested in becoming the first psychologist at the Navy's Basic Underwater Demolition/SEAL training, a.k.a. BUD/S?

This is the training program for incoming Navy SEALs, the sea, air, and land teams that constitute the best of the Navy's best. I said yes, and in September 2006, I left SERE school and joined the BUD/S staff.

My mandate as the BUD/S lead psychologist was twofold. First, I was tasked with creating a psychological assessment mechanism to help identify which candidates were likely to succeed in BUD/S training and which were likely to fail. At the time, BUD/S failure rates (people who didn't complete the training) were 75 percent, which was making it harder for the Navy to achieve its post-9/11 objective of rapidly growing the SEALs. Could I create an assessment system that would help screen out those failures before they even started the training?

Over the next eighteen months my team and I developed, from scratch, a psychological "resilience" test that, when combined with data on the candidate's physical characteristics, became a very good predictor (over 97 percent accuracy) of who would fail BUD/S. We gave the test to all incoming BUD/S classes and used its results to filter out nearly 20 percent of the new trainees. BUD/S completion rates rose from 25 percent to around 40 percent. This was a big win for the program. (People who scored low enough on physical and mental attributes to be filtered out were not permanently rejected. They were given the opportunity to improve and apply again later.)

The assessment tool I developed for BUD/S wasn't about figuring out what was wrong with a person. These were all spectacular individuals, highly mentally and physically fit. There was nothing wrong with any of them. Our job was to help the Navy discern who was mentally prepared to perform at their very best under extreme duress. Unlike many of the existing mental assessment tools available to psychologists, our system wasn't about healing people, it was about predicting performance based on certain psychological attributes, and it worked very well.

My other mandate when I joined BUD/S was to develop a mental toughness curriculum. We developed a tool to assess and predict mental performance. Could we then take the students who passed that test and train them to become even more resilient? Could we train the best to get better? Up until then, the BUD/S program didn't have a codified and teachable mental toughness program. They figured that the extreme and rigorous physical regimen would do the trick. If you can survive SEAL training's infamous Hell Week, the appropriately named highlight of BUD/S training, you must be mentally tough enough, the thinking went. This is only partially true. Yes, students had to be all sorts of mentally and physically tough to survive, but was there a way to better understand the mental tactics and skills they were using to successfully navigate the extreme adversity? And train them to be even tougher? Their resilience was uncanny, but it was learned before they arrived at BUD/S. It became my job to help them hone it.

I started wading into all the available research on the field. For example, in 2006 my British colleagues conducted a seminal study that involved plunging subjects into freezing-cold water. What happens when you jump into water that cold? You gasp, of course! This reflex is involuntary—you can't control it. Except the Brits discovered you can. Their training program, entirely mental, enabled study participants to delay their gasping reflex. After which they were handed a warm towel and a stiff cup of tea.[1]

During the time I was at BUD/S, public interest in the Navy

SEALs and their intense training practices grew substantially, mainly because of their incredible success on the battlefield since 9/11. They were absolutely dominating. There were plenty of TV news stories and magazine articles about BUD/S, often featuring photos of our trainees doing some form of extreme physical exercise (carrying big logs, slogging through the surf in full combat gear) on our San Diego beach.

Famous people started visiting the BUD/S facility, including athletes and teams from the major professional leagues. I was making a career of performance psychology, and here were many of the top performers in the world beating a sandy path to the BUD/S door every day.

So, I made a request to my commanding officer. All these athletes were welcome to come visit, look around, and watch our students train. Our public affairs officer was always fielding visitation inquiries. I had just one request: Would they mind sitting down for an interview with me during their visit? I'd like to ask them a few questions. Like, how do they prepare for upcoming games or matches? And what mental practices made them so resilient and gave them the ability to rise above everyone else to reach the top of their game? What mental skills and techniques do they use to perform under pressure—when it matters most? It will only take an hour or so; would that be OK?

My commanding officer agreed to the request. While they got to visit BUD/S, it was something they could give back to us. They all said yes. Dozens of professional sports teams, US Olympic teams, Lance Armstrong, Michael Phelps, Tiger Woods, and many, many more; every time an athlete came to observe the SEAL training at BUD/S, I got to spend an hour or so interviewing them.

Over time I was able to build an extensive knowledge base of the mental approaches of the world's top performers.

I assimilated this and other research into the first Navy SEAL mental toughness curriculum. But when I reviewed the program with a focus group of SEAL instructors and other experts (talk about a tough focus group!), they weren't so sure about this approach. After all, they had all developed their mental toughness the old-fashioned way: by surviving Hell Week. What good would it be to codify these techniques? By codify, did I mean coddle? So, we compromised: we integrated mental performance techniques into BUD/S training sessions, but during Hell Week no performance psychology coddling was allowed. The students still needed to navigate the stress all by themselves, but at least they would have access to the mental tools and techniques they had learned in BUD/S up to then to help them. And so was born one of the world's first empirically developed military programs focused entirely on mental training to maximize performance.

It took us nearly three years to fully develop and deploy the BUD/S mental toughness program. Once we accomplished that, I shifted my job to become the lead psychologist for all deploying SEAL Teams on the West Coast. In this role, I was able to reinforce the mental performance techniques the SEALs had learned in BUD/S through ongoing practice exercises. While at BUD/S I was training students trying to graduate and become SEALs; now I got to work with active, combat-deploying SEALs. The core competencies of SEALs are shooting, moving, and communicating. This is how they perform, often under mortal threat, and it was my job to help them get better. When they were at BUD/S it's like they were learning their mental toughness ABCs, but once they graduated and joined a SEAL Team they were speaking in sentences. I remained the Naval Special Warfare Group One psychologist from 2009 to 2012, where I worked mainly with SEAL Teams 1, 3, 5, and 7. (There are eight Navy SEAL Teams. Teams 1, 3, 5, and 7 are based in Coronado, California, next to San Diego, while Teams 2, 4, 8, and 10 are based at the Little Creek base in Virginia Beach, Virginia.)

In 2012, I became the force psychologist for the entire SEAL community at Naval Special Warfare Command, a position I held until September 2016, when I retired from the Navy as a commander after twenty years of service. The force psychologist is the lead psychologist for the worldwide SEAL community, responsible for mental health and resiliency, performance optimization, psychological assessment and screening, and research policies and decisions. Today the Navy respects the mental aspects of training for performance as a critical component of selecting, training, and supporting its people. The US is stronger for it.

While still serving in the Navy, I got permission to start working with Red Bull, the sports drink company that sponsors more than 850 athletes across a wide range of sports, from Australian football and BASE jumping to volleyball and wing-suiting. My gig was to help Red Bull develop a new program, the "performing under pressure" (PUP) camps. Think SERE-like training but for extreme athletes. We took elite competitors from a wide variety of sports, threw them together for five-day sessions, and made them experience stress like they had never experienced before. Snake pits and grizzly bears were involved. These exercises included physical challenges, but also emotional ones. Athletes who jump off cliffs may be hard to scare with a physical exercise, but how about getting them up onstage in front of their colleagues and asking them to share an intimate memory? They may not fear dying, but crying is terrifying.

I was the lead psychologist at PUP camps, inoculating hundreds of elite athletes from the stress they regularly experienced in their competitive realms. When you've been chased down a mountain by a grizzly bear (trained to be docile, but they didn't know that!), competing in a world championship doesn't seem like such a big deal. Beyond PUP camp, I was also in charge of all the mental performance programs for Red Bull, which included working as a performance psychologist with the athletes to help them hone their mental game.

In 2015 the Los Angeles Dodgers contacted me. They had toured BUD/S, learned about what we had created, and wanted me to come work with them when I retired from the Navy. When that occurred about a year later, I joined the team as their full-time performance psychologist, helping them build their programs to assess, select, develop, and enhance talent. My team and I built detailed mental performance assessments and curricula for each player in the organization, identifying their strengths and weaknesses from a mental and character perspective to help them be at their best when called upon to perform.

I joined the Dodgers because it was a great opportunity to work with a superb organization and amazing athletes, but also because I grew up an avid Dodger fan! I can still name the starting lineups of most of the teams from about 1975 on, and when I first joined the organization I had to pinch myself when legends such as Steve Garvey, Orel Hershiser, Steve Yeager, and Tommy Lasorda walked past me in the clubhouse.[2] I hit the ground running with the Dodgers, activating mental programs similar to what I had developed for the SEALs, this time for baseball, not battle.

You know that relief pitcher who enters the game in the bottom of the ninth inning with the bases loaded and the game on the line? Chances are that just a few minutes before he walked onto the field, said player was chatting with me near the bullpen, getting centered in the moment, visualizing success, eliminating negative talk, and breathing. Or that heralded draft pick who gets a headline or two before being shipped off to the minors? Chances are I interviewed him and developed a full profile well before the draft. The Dodgers were an incredible organization to work for: an unparalleled ownership group and a visionary president of baseball operations (Andrew Friedman) who drives a culture of innovation, development, data-driven decisions and teamwork. I'd say the combination of these things, coupled with the pre-draft character assessments and the mental performance development and enhancement programs, worked well. During my time with the organization, the Dodgers had the most regular season wins in Major League Baseball, won three National League pennants (the last time they had won one was in 1988), and won the World Series in 2020. Some of my best memories are being showered with champagne by players and staff after Series victories and receiving a World Series ring.

I played a similar role with the US women's national soccer team. Coach Jill Ellis called me before the World Cup tournament in 2019 to see if I could help the team optimize their mental skills and manage the intense pressure they were under to defend their title. I joined the team at their training camps and worked with all the players and coaches, some of them on a weekly basis. I was proud and delighted when Megan Rapinoe, Carli Lloyd, Alex Morgan, and company left France hoisting the World Cup that year.

"HOW CAN I FLIP THIS MENTALLY?"

I also had the privilege of working with dozens of Olympians, including four athletes representing four countries who hauled in a total of eight medals (four gold, three silver, one bronze) at the 2022 Beijing Winter Games. Perhaps the most prominent of those clients was figure skater Nathan Chen. Born and raised in Salt Lake City, Utah, Nathan came by his Olympic aspirations honestly: he was inspired to start skating as a young boy when the 2002 Winter Games were held in his hometown. From there he experienced, with only a few exceptions, nothing but audacious success. With his mother acting as his coach in those early years, he worked his way up through the levels of competition and pushed himself to learn and excel at ever-more-challenging jumps and moves. His commitment to the sport, hard work, and skill took him very far.

As the reigning two-time US champion, Nathan entered the 2018 Winter Olympics in PyeongChang, South Korea, as the overwhelming favorite, with the accompanying hype and pressure. But all that tanked in the first component of the competition, the short program. In a little under three minutes, Nathan went from favorite to failure, flubbing several moves and finishing in seventeenth place. A couple of days later, with the pressure off, he soared in the free-skate component of the competition, notching the highest score in Olympic history. That jumped him up to a fifth-place overall finish, not bad considering his poor start but a massive disappointment nevertheless.

Nathan bounced back from his poor Olympic showing to win the world championships in 2018 and 2019, but in a sport to which many people only pay attention every four years, those victories were not enough to erase the Olympic disappointment. Nathan was determined to try again for Olympic gold. "I needed to find mental coaching," he says, "some mental techniques to put myself in a position to be the best I could be at the games." He was a superb skater, but needed to work on his mental approach to achieve the one accolade that had eluded him: Olympic gold.

We met and got to work starting in June 2021, honing tools such as visualization, self-talk, mindset, and fun. Especially fun, because back in 2018, Nathan wasn't having any. "I don't remember even being there," he says of the PyeongChang Olympics. "I don't remember the flag, I don't remember the dining hall. . . . I was putting in the time, but I didn't enjoy it, I was getting hurt all the time. Generally when I skate I'm present and locked in. I see the colors and the shapes. But in 2018, it was like I wasn't there."

Nathan and I talked a lot about why he skates, why he loves the sport and competing at its highest levels. What did he enjoy as a child? The fun! He had to recapture that joy and remind himself of it at the most critical times. So he "learned to push a mentality of gratitude," Nathan says. "The more I put that into words, the more fun I had. Sometimes I forced myself to say it—I'm so grateful to be here!—even if I didn't feel it. Telling myself these things helped me to remember the happy things about skating, and all the happy times I've had."

These are the practices we discussed frequently over those

months, leading right up to the 2022 Winter Olympic Games in Beijing. Then, just a few hours before the short program began, I got a text from Nathan. I keep making errors on two different elements. How can I set up my mind to do them when it counts? Also, a lot of judges and media coming in. Starting to find myself getting distracted and unable to enjoy as much when I'm feeling critiqued. How can I flip this mentally?

Although I was concerned when I got those texts just before the competition, I was also encouraged. Only a few years before, Nathan thought of skating as a purely physical exercise. Practice the moves, get them right, and victory follows. But now, his questions to me showed he understood it would take mental agility to get those troublesome elements right, not just more ice time. And the jitters experienced as he spotted the judges and media coming in? Also a mental challenge, not a physical one. I knew when I read those texts, half a world away in my San Diego home, that Nathan already knew the answers. He just wanted to hear them from me.

I started by reminding him (via text) to visualize his program, especially the troublesome moves. I wrote back: Visualize them successfully completed, using as many senses as possible. Your brain will wire those success connections in.

As for those annoying judges and media? I told him [they] are merely passengers along with YOUR experience. Just tell yourself they are no different than random people watching one of your practices from the high seats. This is about your experience, not their narrative. You've loved skating and creating on the ice since you were a child. Just be you out there. This experience is only yours.

Remember, emotions are contagious, I concluded. Your

body will follow what your emotions are. Create emotions of fun, excitement, happiness . . . like an energized, loose, and happy practice. The body will follow.

OK very helpful. Thanks very much! Nathan responded, then I didn't hear from him again. Had my advice worked? I got a clue when I turned on my TV to watch the competition. The cameras followed Nathan in the athletes' warm-up area. Like many of the skaters, he was visualizing his program, eyes closed, headphones on, body miming some of the moves he would soon be making on the ice. I had seen this many times before, but this time there was something a bit different. Nathan was laughing! Not a lot, not very loud, but several times as he moved through his own world, he encountered something that made him smile.

"I think that was natural," he said later when I asked him about the smiles. "I was consciously trying to make myself have fun. This is what I trained for, I told myself, and regardless of how it goes, I want to have this opportunity."

And boy did he. A Chinese American man skating in his mother's home city, billions watching around the globe, rigid COVID protocols, a very challenging program, having invested four years to wipe away the memory of a three-minute skate gone bad, performs at his absolute best and wins going away. In fact, except for members of the military and first responders I've worked with and seen in action, his short-program performance was one of the greatest, if not the greatest, human performances I've ever seen. Nathan Chen is a superior athlete and person, with a sharp intellect, boundless humility, exhausting work ethic, and well-grounded values. Everything he has achieved in life, on and off the ice, is a direct result of those characteristics. I merely guided him to discover the mental performance techniques required to be his very best. Actualizing those techniques was all his doing.

In our time working together, Nathan learned and excelled at several mental performance techniques: visualization, detailed mindset preparation, positive self-talk, and focusing only on what he can control. But underlying all of these tactics was the fundamental principle of fun and its close relative, purpose. Why do we perform? Yes, the outcomes matter: the trophies, medals, paychecks, and rewards. But what really motivates us is internal. Meaning, purpose, and joy are not tied to judges and rankings and things. They are within us. They are intrinsic. To become an Olympic champion, Nathan had to forget about becoming an Olympic champion and remember to have fun.

How did that go? "In Beijing, I had a suite with three of my closest friends from the team. I brought my guitar with me. I would play for an hour and not realize the time had gone by. I really enjoyed it. I had fun!" And he won.

Enough about me. Let's get to work. Are you ready to learn excellence?

CHAPTER 3

Values and Goals

I started thinking that I was a human
first and diver second. For the first time
in my career, I was able to completely
overcome the phenomenon of reputation.

—David Colturi, competitive cliff diver

David Colturi used to worry about his reputation, which is kind of crazy for a guy who makes his living diving off cliffs. Yes, there is such a thing as professional cliff diving. Organized by Red Bull, the "World Series" of cliff diving hosts dozens of events around the world every year. Divers leap from a small platform, usually built atop a cliff but occasionally on bridges and buildings, set at heights of about 27 meters (88 feet). They hit the water at a speed of over 50 mph. When he's diving, David has plenty of things to worry about besides his reputation.

"You're up there at about ninety feet, that's about the height of an eight-story building," David says in describing the experience. "When you step to the edge and look down, the safety divers are specks. Like ants on the water." Reading David's description, anybody with a fear of heights (or who is sane) might develop a sense of apprehension. You are feeling your fear. David feels it, too. "That's when my natural primal fear instinct kicks in, the fight-or-flight response. Fear is a necessary thing. It's not about the absence of fear, it's about controlling the fear."

Growing up in Ohio, David was active in many sports, but he fully committed to springboard and platform diving in high school. (Springboards are up to three meters above the water. Platforms are up to ten.) David excelled at the 10-meter platform events, winning the individual and synchronized US national men's championship in those events in 2009. By then he had started diving from even greater heights; a summer job in an amusement park water show had him dropping off a 20-meter platform! He went to Purdue University and took pre-med courses, planning to go to med school to further his interest in studying the limits of human performance, but then he decided to learn about those limits firsthand rather than academically. By diving off cliffs. He qualified for the Red Bull World Series in 2012, the youngest diver ever to do so.

Along the way David's coaches introduced him to many mental skills, such as mindset, visualization, and compartmentalization, but these lessons didn't really take. "I was super emotional," David recalls. "I was concerned with other people's opinions, and all the distractions and noise, I didn't have the ability to shut them out. So, when my coaches introduced me to the tools, I couldn't commit to them."

David and I first started working together in April 2016. At the time, he was a tactician, a very skilled diver who did a good job employing the mental techniques he had been taught, such as visualization. But he focused a lot on reputation and let his emotions get in the way too often. My initial assessment found that he possessed lower emotional control, higher negative self-talk, and lower scores on automaticity, which is the ability to trust one's training and go on "autopilot" during a performance. People who score low on automaticity tend to overthink upcoming performances, which can lead to action paralysis, anxiety, and self-doubt. Not exactly what you want when you are about to dive off a ninety-foot cliff into the water below. When it's go time like that, you want to empty your mind and trust your training.

In the summer of 2018, David was competing in an event in Sisikon, Switzerland, a village on the shore of Lake Lucerne. To help promote the event he agreed to do a "teaser dive," where the diver comes out a few days before the event and performs a stunt dive to generate interest. In David's case, the stunt involved diving from a tiny platform suspended from a paraglider. Because diving from a cliff isn't hard enough. David and the pilot took off from a nearby hill, soared over the lake, and at the right spot David leapt from the platform.

The first attempt wasn't great. Determined to get it right for the cameras, David and the pilot tried again. "On the second attempt," David says, "we came in super high and slow. I stood up and was ready to go. I'm thinking we're too high, and then as soon as I jump, I know it. I think we were at about a hundred and fifteen feet. Right before I hit the water—I was about to belly flop—I turned so I could take the impact on my side. I almost lost consciousness. We thought about canceling the project, but I'm stubborn. I really wanted to do this and get it right."

So up they went again, and on the third and fourth attempts they got it right. In videos of the dive available online, David can be seen executing a clean somersault and feetfirst entry, then surfacing with a big smile and wave. A few hours later he collapsed. His spleen, it turns out, had been badly lacerated by the impact with the water during the second dive. He was rushed to the hospital, where an emergency splenectomy saved his life.

The next day David woke up in the ICU, his surgeon telling him he was lucky to be alive. His grandmother called him and asked: "You are definitely done with this cliff diving, right?" That's when David realized he was determined to dive again, that he could come back even stronger and better. He was disappointed to let his grannie down, but excited to get to work on recovery.

While the crash in Switzerland wasn't exactly an epiphany for David, it did provide him an opportunity to fully immerse himself in the mental performance work we had started a couple of years earlier. His main challenge: to shift from valuing reputation to valuing identity. To do that, he needed to figure out that identity.

WHO ARE YOU?

It's a simple question, right? You will probably answer with your name and maybe your profession (if you're an adult) or what year you are in school and where you go (if you're a student). You could add a detail or two about where you're from and whether you are married or single, and perhaps provide your preferred pronouns.

None of which gets to the real you: humans are far too complicated to be a simple answer to a simple question. You aren't your name, profession, school, hometown, or gender. Those are a part of you, but they don't define you. You are an embodied set of emotions, thoughts, experiences, knowledge, wisdom, and values. Much more than a who-are-you answer.

Learning excellence starts with developing a deeper understanding of ourselves: how we act, why we act that way, and what drives us. That's why, when I start working with someone who wants to optimize their performance, we begin with the development of a personal credo as the necessary foundation for building excellence. It's a short statement consisting of the ten words that define their identity. These "identity markers" constitute the core of what you care about, enjoy, embody, and live for. We get to it by asking a few powerful questions. The first is the one that elite performers learn to *not* ask themselves: What do people think of you?

This one gets your mind racing, doesn't it? Maybe it incites a bit of anxiety. You will probably answer by saying, "I hope they think . . ." followed by a series of positive things that, in your ideal world, people use to describe you. Then you sigh and say, "But they probably think . . ." followed by a series of less positive things that, in your realistic world, people use to describe you. You hope they think the positive things; you worry they don't.

In fact, you do more than just worry. If you are like most humans, you spend more time fretting about what others think about you (reputation) than you do on your own values, motivation, and goals (identity). This is a problem for performers: in my experience, the ones who are preoccupied with reputation—colleagues and coworkers, social media, competition, stakeholders—don't do as well. When we work to re-vector attention away from reputation and toward identity, performance improves.

Where we stand on the reputation versus identity spectrum evolves. As young kids, we are all about identity. Whether we are playing, running, dancing, or even throwing a tantrum, our actions are unbiased by what others think of us. This isn't to say that as young children we are selfish—in fact, kindness and generosity are frequently components of our identity. It's just that we don't much care about what others think. But soon we start to care. We stop playing, running, and dancing with abandon (most of us, anyway), and turn our concerns to reputation. By our teenage years it absorbs us, a situation amplified by social media. We are relentlessly told and shown what success is and what happiness looks like, rather than drawing those insights from ourselves. It's not what we care about, it's what *they* care about. This can lead to performance anxiety: lower confidence, reduced ambition, and that incessant, nagging voice in the head that won't shut up.

Caring about reputation is one type of extrinsic motivator; it derives its benefit from something external, whereas intrinsic motivators come from within. There is research evidence that intrinsic motivators are more powerful than extrinsic ones, which in practice means that digging into intrinsic motivators, such as identity, can crowd out the extrinsic motivator of reputation. Of course things are more complicated than simply intrinsic > extrinsic or identity > reputation, but what is clear from my experience is that, left to its own devices, reputation anxiety can consume performers, even those you think wouldn't be susceptible to it.

Pete Naschak was a Navy SEAL for twenty-one years, rising to become the command master chief of SEAL Team 5, with up to five hundred SEALs, sailors, and soldiers under his leadership during their combat deployment in Iraq. (The CMC is the senior enlisted leader at a command, working as its top adviser for the commanding officer, senior training and tactical expert, and liaison for the enlisted ranks and their families.) Today, Pete still remembers how his concern for reputation got in his way early in his SEAL career. "In training, I was sometimes more focused on not wanting to do something wrong. I wondered what others would think. I didn't want to mess up and affect my reputation."

The good news is, when you stay true to identity, reputation takes care of itself. I have seen this played out over and over. A strong performer starts reading those online comments or pandering to what they think their audience or colleagues want, and things start to tank. When the same performer learns to ignore reputation and embrace identity: better results, happier person. The trick is to shift concerns of reputation into reminders of identity. Be true to yourself and good stuff will happen. This requires a deeper understanding of self than most people have. It's not hard to develop, but it does take time.

The personal credo is a foundation and process to refocus from reputation to identity. Developing it is not a quick exercise; if you think you are done after an hour of reflection, think again. Rather, once you decide to draft your credo, take the time over the next few weeks to notice the things that bring you energy, joy, motivation, and excitement. What are those characteristics or attributes that best describe you at your core? Notice what you care about, and in those moments jot down a word or two to describe the value at the core of that emotion you are feeling. These could be big things but also small. If a good meal brings you joy, take a moment to think about why that is. Sure, it tastes good, but there is probably something deeper there.

Be expansive in this process; you are going to cull the list later, so it's OK to throw a few things at the wall just to see if they stick. Toby Miller, a professional snowboarder with whom I have worked, notes that "when we first discussed creating my personal credo, I thought, This is going to be easy. I know who I am. But the second I started writing them down I realized I couldn't come up with ten words. All of it was about snowboarding. I realized I'm a brother, a boyfriend, a son. The biggest takeaway was that I'm an athlete, not just a snowboarder, and this helped me find new passions I loved." (Toby was all of twenty-two years old when he said this.) He ended up developing the following credo: *Be motivated, supportive, appreciative, curious, adventurous, positive, precise, humble, organized.*

Once you have developed this list of identity markers, the next step is to consolidate it down to ten words or fewer. While this number is somewhat arbitrary, the exercise of culling the list is valuable in itself, as it will push you to prioritize and go deeper. Why is this a value of mine? Which of these markers feel the best to me, which are the things I want to double and triple down on? Which excite me the most?

When you have drafted your list, ask a few people with whom you are close to write down their version of your personal credo. What do they think you value? They don't need to take weeks to do this; just thirty to sixty minutes of quiet thinking should suffice. When they share the list with you, see what overlaps with your list and what new things pop up. When I did this with my wife and a couple of friends, they all noted my value of not being complacent: I don't like to settle! This was already on my list, but they also noted my sense of humor, which I hadn't included.

Throughout this process, be honest with yourself. I've seen clients start with items such as "win at any cost," "be a billionaire," "uneasy," and "dissatisfied," things that they might not feel comfortable broadly sharing. That's fine; the whole point of the exercise is to take a look in the mirror and discern who you are. In some cases (like "be a billionaire"), you can dig into the values beneath them. Others may be fine as is: my client who claimed "uneasy" and "dissatisfied" as part of their core used those values as fuel to get better. This self-exploration helps you learn more about who you are. And your values are not etched in stone; they evolve as you grow older and your life changes.

When I tasked David Colturi with developing his personal credo after his accident, he asked himself what people would say at his funeral and what he wanted them to say as a way of gauging the legacy he was going to leave behind. Was it something he would be proud of? It took some time, and there was no particular "aha moment." Gradually, a more complete self-portrait emerged, words that not only represented his credo, but became the building blocks of his identity: *selfless, discipline, grit, mindful, stoic, clarity, character, courage,* ikigai, *evolving.*

David lost his Red Bull sponsorship about the same time as the accident. This was not just a blow to his finances; it was a blow to his identity. "I had to realize I was so much more than David Colturi, Red Bull cliff diver. I am still a worthwhile and amazing human being outside those things." As the weeks and months went by, David became more comfortable in his skin—he was at peace. "I started thinking that I was a human first and diver second. For the first time in my career, I was able to completely overcome the phenomenon of reputation."

He thought more about what he enjoyed and what he didn't, and started to avoid the latter. Sounds simple, right? I enjoy ice cream so I eat that; I don't like baby bok choy so I avoid that. But how about that party invitation, the one offered by the friend of the friend whom you don't really know? You don't want to go, but you "should," because what will people think if you aren't there? David had been in that situation many times, but after he stopped worrying so much about what others thought, he started to say no more often. Now he acts based on identity rather than reputation.

None of this was easy. "Not caring about your reputation, what others think, is superhuman," David says. "The experience of almost dying gave me a fresh perspective. I got a lot more determination, more grit. It took work to learn about my character. I learned to stop focusing energy on the wrong things. It was life changing for me." The accident was a catalyst, providing an opportunity for David to unpack, explore, and sharpen his mental approach. He emerged as someone with contagious kindness and mind-blowing discipline; calm, balanced, and identity-based. His automaticity is much higher; he's back atop the ninety-foot cliffs, thinking less and diving better.

I refer to my personal credo so often that I can recite it without even thinking: *Wonder, stay hungry, stay humble, stay connected, loyalty, listen, laugh.* I have used it to guide every important decision of my life, and I counsel my clients to do the same.

Blaine Vess is an entrepreneur and investor with whom I started working in 2020. In 1999 he cofounded a company, Student Brands, with a friend. Blaine was a freshman in college at the time,

and started the company as a way to share course notes and research online. His parents had told him that life's not always about
fun, but when he and his colleagues graduated from college and
moved into a house in Los Angeles together, in fact they had a
lot of fun. They also worked hard and persevered through a lot of
ups and downs before eventually selling the company to Barnes &
Noble Education in 2017.

Blaine and I worked together on things like setting goals and
compartmentalization, but it was the process of developing his
credo (*Freedom, patience, authenticity, fun, entrepreneurship, growth
mindset, give back, self-awareness, community, humility*) that has
been most important for him. "My credo has been huge," he says.
"Out of all of its attributes, the one that stands out is fun. With
anything I do I'll push myself to think big, but then I think I
should slow down and remember to have fun." Now he uses his
credo to guide his strategy as he invests in dozens of start-ups.

Ted Brown is another good example. Ted is a producer and
president at Lockton Denver, a large risk management and employee benefits firm. Ted's title is fancy, but what's more impressive
is that he is one of Lockton's top producers, having built invaluable relationships with dozens of business clients. In his field, Ted
is a world-class performer at the top of his game. Even with that
fancy title, Ted, as he tells me, still loves to "go out and earn new
business."

I started working with Ted in 2018, by which time he was already very successful. His corner of the insurance industry is hy-
percompetitive, and reputation counts more than in most jobs.
Companies are putting their risk and exposure in your hands, so
they need to trust and believe in you at a deeply personal level. But

even in this environment where reputation actually counts, to be his best self Ted had to stop worrying about it. He and I worked on shifting focus from reputation to identity.

After months of iteration, Ted developed his credo: *Family, grit, servant leader, team, authenticity, competition, sacrifice, performance, and love.* These identity markers became his daily focus and the lens by which he started to view everything, both at Lockton and at home. The results were dramatic. The average compounded annual growth rate at Lockton is 12 percent; Ted's hit 36 percent after we started working together. "I finally started to focus on what is truly important to me and not worry about my reputation," Ted recalls. Then he laughs and says, "My reputation is probably better now than it has ever been!"

Anchoring on a well-conceived values credo can be more than just a basis for mental performance practice: it can be life critical. Andy Walshe spent nearly nine years running the high-performance program at Red Bull, working with hundreds of elite athletes and artists. He discovered an interesting twist on the importance of performers having a personal credo: "You need a meaning and purpose in life to excel," he explains. "If all you live for is to become the best in the world, it leaves you short once you *become* the best in the world. If who you are is what you do, then you are setting yourself up to be in harm's way. At some point you aren't going to be number one. High performance is extraordinary, but for most people, it's only a phase in their life. You can't perform at the top of the game forever. We want to get them to number one, but at the same time we want to help them with what happens next. We do that by bringing connection back to other human values. To create a better you: human, teammate, member of a community."

Your credo reflects and codifies who you are. Creating and reading it helps create that connection Andy references. It is powerful, because there is something energizing about knowing and performing as yourself. Identity can be counted on. Reputation can't.

WHAT ARE YOUR GOALS?

When Carli Lloyd was nine years old, she made a list. She was heading off to soccer camp and the list, diligently recorded in her notebook and discovered in a box in the attic by grown-up Carli many years later, included the things she wanted to learn at the camp. This wasn't an unusual occurrence; quite the opposite. Little Carli was the queen of list making. She also made a list that said when she grew up she wanted to be rich, famous, and fast. The list did not include being a mainstay of the US women's soccer team that won two FIFA World Cups (2015, 2019) and two Olympic gold medals (2008, 2012), and being named FIFA player of the year (2015, 2016). If it had, she would have checked off every item.

It would be an overstatement to say that Carli's huge success was a result of her penchant for creating lists, but "setting goals and writing them down is a huge part of how I got to where I am today," she says. "That process has never changed. I still write down overall goals—I want to learn these maneuvers, I want to achieve this at practice." And they aren't just goals related to soccer. "I make life goals, too." Such as? "Countries I want to visit. Quotes and excerpts from books. Things I want to learn. There's always something to learn."

Creating a goal is a good start, but there are three additional steps in the goal-setting process to up the chances of success:

- Write it down.
- Publicly commit (by sharing it with others).
- Create an accountability plan.

Writing it down is a big step. The act of codifying a goal immediately creates accountability; now that it has a physical presence, you have to make it happen. Sharing the goal with others—friends, colleagues, family—ratchets accountability up even more. Once you tell people you're going to do something, now you really have to make it happen. And having a plan to accomplish the goal and track your progress is just common sense. A 2015 study led by psychologist Gail Matthews corroborates this goal-setting hierarchy: people who merely thought about their goals achieved them (or were well on their way to success) 43 percent of the time, writing the goals down boosted that rate to 62 percent, and sharing the goals and regular progress updates with a friend cranked it to 76 percent.

(A well-known 1953 study of Yale University graduates found that only 3 percent of them had written goals upon graduation. Twenty years later those 3 percent had accumulated more wealth than the other 97 percent combined. This study was taught for years in psychology graduate programs, including mine, as an example of the power of goal setting. Unfortunately, a 1996 *Fast Company* article researched the research and concluded the famous Yale study never happened. It may have been well-known, but it was also a myth. This inspired Matthews to conduct her own study, which corroborated many of the findings of the Yale legend. Except for the wealth part!)

Creating a credo helps anchor a performer. Setting and writing down goals help that performer become excellent. I have my clients do this across six aspects of their lives: career, relationships, health, spirituality, hobbies, and legacy. The prompt I use: One, three, and six months from now, what do you want to be true in each area?

Set specific, nonfuzzy goals that are easy to understand and easy to measure. When they set their goals, Navy SEALs employ the "SMART" framework. A good goal should be specific, measurable (you will know when you have achieved it), achievable (it's feasible for you to get there), relevant (it matters), and timebound (achieved within a specified period). So, "I will get in better shape" is not a SMART goal, but "I will be able to jog six miles in under an hour by December so I'll be ready for my winter basketball league" is.

Process-oriented goals are at least as valuable and effective as outcome-oriented ones. It's fine to set an ambitious outcome as a goal, but for every outcome goal ("make VP by age thirty-five" or "run a marathon in under four hours"), it's a good idea to establish a process goal as well ("spend an hour a day studying the business" or "alternate short- and long-distance runs and train with weights once per week"). Amateurs focus on outcome, professionals focus on process. (More on that in chapter 5.)

Like setting a personal credo, developing meaningful goals in six aspects of life should be a thoughtful, iterative process. Don't just quickly jot something down so you can knock the last thing off your to-do list before finishing work on a random Tuesday.

Take time, write them down, leave it for a while, then come back to it.

Keep in mind that the most achievable goals are intrinsic, not extrinsic. People are far more motivated to achieve goals that are based on their values (intrinsic) than those based on what other people think (extrinsic). The goal isn't to score a bunch of likes on your YouTube video or Instagram post; it's to enjoy what you were doing when you made the video or photo. (I know, crazy.) The nine-year-old Carli Lloyd didn't set a goal to learn a particular maneuver in soccer camp because someone told her she needed to or because she thought her teammates would be impressed; she set that goal because it was what *she* wanted.

To ensure a goal is intrinsic, ask why it's a goal. If the goal is to lose ten pounds, why? Is it because someone said you look out of shape (extrinsic), or because you want to feel better and healthier (intrinsic)? For each goal you create, explore why that goal is important. This simple process of inquiry will yield far more meaningful goals.

Thomas Edison is quoted as saying, "To have a good idea, have a lot of them." (The quote is also attributed Nobel laureate Linus Pauling, who may have also added "To have a good quote, say the same thing as Thomas Edison.") The same does not apply to goals. It is better to have a few good goals than a bunch of mediocre ones. One per area is good for starters. You can always add more, and keeping things simple helps ensure your resources are more tightly focused. But achieving those goals should not be as easy as flipping on and off a light switch (the ease of which was one of Edison's ideas). Excellence doesn't come easy. Good goals should be realistic but challenging.

In my experience, people struggle the most with goal setting in the spiritual aspect of their lives. When I bring up spirituality, people immediately go to religion. If they aren't religious (and sometimes even if they are), they struggle to come up with a goal. But spirituality isn't about religion and being closer to your deity and doctrine of choice; it's about coming in touch with your humanity. What does it mean to be human, to have feelings? What are you beyond your physical being? Dude, these are big questions! You can choose to make God and religion part of your answers and your goals, such as committing to attend religious services, but spiritual goals could also include things like meditation, mindfulness, or yoga (which is meditation and mindfulness while standing on your head). Spirituality is embedded in these activities.

Giving yourself the space to ask and reflect upon your spirituality can be a goal in itself. Many of the performers I have worked with are young and fearless and have never taken the time to truly investigate their own humanity and spirituality. Many people include meditation and "being more present" as a goal, which is fine, but remember to ask why. If those are your goals because they are many people's goals, start over.

Toby Miller, the pro snowboarder, sounds like he's practically channeling Carli Lloyd when he talks about his goal-setting practices. "At a young age," he says, "I would write down all the tricks I wanted to learn. I recently found a list I made when I was ten! That process hasn't changed. I still write down overall goals, the maneuvers I want to learn. I have specific goals for each camp. I write them down and bring the list with me. If I'm having a bad day, I use my goals to turn it into a good day. There's always something I can learn."

WHAT IS YOUR ENGINE?

In March 2009, the New York Yankees invited me to come to their spring training camp in Tampa, Florida, to address players, coaches, and staff about the mental characteristics and practices of elite performers. A week or so later, I walked into the Yankee clubhouse a couple of hours before a game and was astonished to see not just the current roster (which included superstars Derek Jeter and Alex Rodriguez) but many iconic Yankee greats from the past, such as Reggie Jackson, Goose Gossage, and Yogi Berra. I grew up a baseball fan, so I knew I was surrounded by the game's royalty. A little nervous, I launched into my talk. This was a few years after my team and I had developed the first mental toughness curriculum for the Navy SEALs, so that's what I covered that day.

When my talk concluded, I gathered my stuff and started to walk out as the players turned to the game at hand. That's when Yogi Berra tracked me down. "Great talk, Doc, I loved it," he said, "but can I add something to what you talked about?"

Could he add something to what I talked about? Yogi Berra was the Yankee catcher from 1946 through 1963, winning ten world championships and three Most Valuable Player awards and appearing in eighteen All-Star Games during that stretch. He followed his playing career with many successful years as a major-league coach and manager, and was elected to the Baseball Hall of Fame in 1972. And he was the inspiration for the "smarter than the average bear" cartoon character, Yogi Bear. (Yogi—the person—passed away in 2015.) So yeah, he could add something. As Yogi is quoted as saying, "When you see a fork in the road, take it." I took the fork and said that I would be honored to hear what he had to say.[1]

He made his comments short and sweet. He told me he had played with and coached many great players, and they all were motivated by something. He called it their "engine." He had seen many different motivations among those players, with the most prevalent being the motivations to not lose and to win (which are not the same thing). But regardless of what the motivation was, every player had something they were playing for.

Yogi's words, while not reaching the legendary status of other Yogi-isms, had an immediate effect on me. While I had paid attention to motivation in my work up to then, I found his conviction around this topic quite impactful. After that, I always made it a point to take a deeper dive into my clients' motivating factors. Years later, I came across a couple of Yogi quotes that brought me back to that day in the Yankee spring training clubhouse. "Losing's a great motivator," said the man who mostly avoided it during his playing career. And, "If you don't know where you're going, you might not get there."

To help get there, a better question than "What motivates you?" might be "What is your engine?" Learning to be excellent is all about that engine and what fuels it. What is your engine? Is it money? Fame? Recognition? Success? Winning? Not losing? Vanity? Love? Hate? If your answer to this question is simple (money, fame, status), ask yourself another question: Why? Why do I care about money or fame? Why does that promotion mean so much to me? There are often deeper motivations at play, and it helps to understand them.

There is a nuanced difference between motivation (your engine) and values (your credo). The engine is what motivates you; the credo is what you care about at your core. For example, someone who grew up financially insecure may be motivated by money and value security. People who value ambition will be motivated by success and its trappings. Competitiveness as a value is correlated with winning as a motivator. When I first start working with clients, I ask them to think about their credo, which requires thought and reflection and is often an enlightening experience. This process can entail looking at motivators, which are usually more obvious, and examining the connection between motivators and values. Optimal performance happens when motivators and values are aligned: the things that drive you are based on your core values. This isn't always the case; sometimes we discover that the things that drive us are misaligned with our values. Maybe we crave that new car or promotion because of external factors rather than internal ones. When such misalignment occurs, people often end up rethinking their engine.

WHAT IS THE HARDEST THING YOU'VE EVER EXPERIENCED?

In 2000, I was asked to provide subject matter expertise testimony in a forensic case. I was nervous about being asked difficult questions from the opposing attorney. How would I respond if they asked me questions like, "In your professional opinion, is this person likely to behave this way in the future?" How could I provide a professional opinion on the likelihood of a particular future behavior?

I talked to my friend and mentor, Dr. Bill Perry, about my concerns. Bill has been my mentor since we met in 1994. A renowned clinical neuropsychologist, he was my dissertation chair, guiding me through the process of getting my doctorate degree, and has been invaluable in guiding my professional development. He answered that day with a nugget of wisdom I recall frequently. "The best predictor of future behavior is past behavior," Bill said. "If someone asks you if someone will do something in the future, the best response is to ask if they have done it in the past." People can and do change, but past behavior is typically a good predictor of future behavior. Sage advice, well grounded with a large body of research.[2]

Much of excellence is about performing well under stress: the job interview, the speech, the big meeting or performance. How you perform under stress, in those times of challenge and controversy, is part of who you are. This is why, in my initial session with someone, I always ask them, "What is the hardest thing you've experienced?" This can be a challenging and emotional query; responses I've heard include the death of a loved one, a divorce or breakup, a failed exam or course, bankruptcy, rejection, a loss in a big game, an accident, or being fired or laid off. There is no right answer; we've all gone through situations that deeply test us.

Next, I'll ask the more important question: How did you navigate that situation? This is telling, as someone is likely to apply the same strategies and tactics they used for the previous hard thing to the next hard thing. Your response might have been healthy (used internal coping skills, talked the situation through with friends or family, accessed other support systems in your community), unhealthy, (alcohol or substance abuse, lashing out, casting blame, going into isolation), human (freaked out, started crying or yelling), or some mix of all three. Recall the event or time, and how you behaved and felt. If it helps, write this down, set it aside, then revisit and iterate upon it. Again, there's no right answer other than being honest with yourself.

Recalling how you handled things—did you fight, flee, or freeze—gives you a good indication of what will happen the next time the stress dials up. Whether you are already cool under pressure, or you break out into a sweat and pant like a dog at the slightest tension, understanding that baseline of behavior sets a platform upon which you can build and grow. Character is revealed by adversity. (Martin Luther King Jr.: "The ultimate measure of a man is not where he stands in moments of comfort and convenience, but where he stands at times of challenge and controversy.") Asking the hardest thing question is a way of holding up a mirror to show people a pattern of behavior they may not recognize. It can be powerful and enlightening.

Hard things and adversity are part of life, regardless of your life stage, profession, family status, or anything else. Stuff happens. It will happen again. The best performers don't have a secret way of avoiding these things, nor are they somehow wired from birth to keep it cool. Rather, they learn what their default response is, then work to improve on it (more on that in subsequent chapters).

KNOWING WHY YOU ARE IN THE BUILDING

You can use the questions I present in this chapter to understand who you are, what you care about, how you manage pressure, and what you want to achieve. When things go wrong or challenges seem too daunting, it's easy to crumble. The performers who have taken the time and intellectual and spiritual energy to learn about themselves are the ones with the fortitude to persevere. They intrinsically know who they are, what they are doing, and why, and never have to question it.

When Erik Spoelstra first sent me an out-of-the-blue email in May 2016, he was already a tremendously successful NBA coach. Hired by the Miami Heat in 2008 as one of the youngest coaches in NBA history, Erik subsequently led the team to four straight Finals appearances (2011–14), winning titles in 2012 and 2013. "When I became head coach, I was very results oriented, which brought a lot of pressure and anxieties," Erik says. "Then we signed the big three [superstars LeBron James, Chris Bosh, and Dwyane Wade joined the Heat in 2010], and it really became about results."

Erik's results were very good. Still, at the conclusion of that four-year Finals run, he was exhausted. "I was empty, lost. I took six weeks away from the team to evaluate things. I set out to find a deeper purpose in my job." Erik needed to get back to his identity, and he needed to guide his team and organization to find theirs as well. He wanted to lead his team through core values, things like teamwork, trust, vulnerability, and accountability. That this need was compelled not by the pressure of failure but by the pressure of success didn't matter. The need was very real, and it's part of what led Erik on the path to seek me out.

When Erik sent me that email, he asked if we could meet during an upcoming trip to San Diego. A few weeks later we sat down for lunch at one of my favorite cafés in Coronado. He told me he wanted to keep learning and to have his players be exposed to as many mental tactics as possible. He had been researching the work I and others had done around mental toughness training, including my program at BUD/S, and he wanted more. We spent a couple of hours outlining how to embed mental performance into the team and organizational culture. He offered me an ongoing consulting engagement and invited me to attend the Heat's training camp the following September. The next day I received a text from him: The most interesting lunch. Uncharted waters. I'm very intrigued and want to help our players in a more powerful way.

A few months later Andrea and I arrived at the Heat training camp in the Bahamas. Over the course of the next week, while Andrea enjoyed the island, I got to work with the coaching staff and all the players. I gave mental performance presentations, built profiles, met with each player, and attended practices. The players and staff, led by Erik, were hungry to learn anything and everything they could to improve above the neck and between the ears. He brought me in not just to help the team win, but to help it build on its culture of excellence, a journey he had started after that 2014 Finals loss. "I have a great responsibility and take great pride in being a caretaker for this culture," Erik says. "We're trying to compete for a championship; it's all about winning. That goes without saying. But there is an emptiness to that."

Erik understands that it is the team's values and culture that matter the most. "I am the steward and caretaker of this culture. Every time I come into the building I know why I'm here. If you get away from your process and values you get lost."

LEARNED EXCELLENCE ACTION PLAN—VALUES AND GOALS

TO KNOW YOURSELF AND WHY YOU ARE "IN THE BUILDING," WRITE A PERSONAL CREDO THAT CAPTURES YOUR CORE VALUES.

Develop long-term (one-, three-, and six-month) goals across six aspects of your life.

Figure out what your "engine" is, the things about which you are most passionate, and dig to understand the relationship between your motivators and values.

Understand your stress response by recalling your hardest experience and how you handled it.

CHAPTER 4

Mindset

What is there to learn from this? Every setback, failure, or rejection has yielded different answers to the question.

—Katy Stanfill, former naval officer and pilot

Katy Stanfill is an achiever. She played on the soccer team while at the US Naval Academy and was a good student, earning a berth at Aviation Training School in Pensacola, Florida (a.k.a. flight school) after graduation. Still, she was always, in her own words, "a bit shy—assertiveness was something I had to learn." Her robust record of excellence, was, counterintuitively, indicative of an underlying lack of confidence. "Achievement was what I leaned towards. I found I could lean on competency more than confidence."

Confident or not, Katy's mindset was working for her. In flight school she specialized in helicopters, and when it came time to choose which model she would fly upon completing her training, she chose the oldest model in the Navy fleet, the Vietnam-era CH-46 Sea Knight. Used for supply and search-and-rescue missions, the CH-46 was an "egg beater" with two rotors on top but none on the tail. The one many of us have seen in movies.

Why choose such an outdated machine? Perhaps it was Katy's penchant for challenges and achievement. "The jet pilots had the best grades, but that wasn't me. Choosing this helo was about not wanting to rely on technology, and wanting to be a 'good stick.' I always had a deep sense of trying to prove myself. I was the underdog, a female in a male world, a quiet leader. I was very determined, almost rigid in my mind. I'm going to do this. I like a challenge, I like how it feels on the other side."

During flight school, Katy had to successfully complete a round in the "helo dunker," where she was strapped into a helicopter cockpit alongside her crew, then dropped into a large pool and flipped upside down (helicopters are top-heavy so tend to capsize in water), all the while wearing darkened goggles to simulate nighttime conditions. Because, you know, doing the exercise during the day would be too easy. "Lots of people panic," Katy says blithely. She didn't.

(Right about now you are probably saying "that sounds terrifying!" It is. I completed my own helo dunker swim in the mid-1990s as part of my ongoing training regimen. It scared the hell out of me. It's disorienting enough to be strapped inside a helicopter cockpit next to others, then dunked and flipped. But add the darkness goggles and things get really scary. You have to blindly feel your way out, along with other members of the crew, without losing your cool. There are divers in the pool, only a few feet away, ready to save anyone who needs it, but in the moment it is easy to forget that. I got through it, though, and after that my subsequent flights in aircraft such as F/A-18, S-3, and EA-6 were relatively easy.)

After flight school, Katy completed SERE training (later she became an instructor at SERE, which is when we met), so by the time she headed out for her first deployment she was fully inoculated to handle stress. Anyone who goes through the helo dunker and SERE school has been subjected to the most stressful situations possible, and Katy successfully navigated them. It's not that she was immune to stress; rather she was armed with tools to manage it. She was ready for anything that might come her way.

Nevertheless, her first deployment didn't start well. She was at sea performing her first real "vertical replenishment" mission, which involves moving cargo between two ships via helicopter. As Katy descended toward a Navy ship carrying a heavy load of cargo, the flight controls suddenly felt rigid and unresponsive. This was a very dangerous situation, with both the helicopter and people on the deck seconds away from potential disaster. Her crewman unhooked the load as the helicopter jerked away so there was no harm done, except to her belief in herself.

"My confidence was shot," she says. When she returned to the carrier to land, "I couldn't bring myself to fly the helicopter close to the landing pad." Eventually she had to hand off control to her copilot, who landed successfully. They checked out the equipment: everything was working properly. Whatever problems they had encountered were likely due to pilot error.

"What was broken was up here," Katy says, tapping her temple. "I felt a lot of shame. I had spent years preparing for this! Yet I couldn't bring myself to get the helicopter close enough to land." She pauses, then wonders, "What got me through that?"

Katy had gotten to this point by being an achiever focused on outcome, and it had worked because the outcomes had gone her way. But now she had failed, in a public and dangerous way, and when she tried again all she could think about was that failure. It's a hard thing, landing a load of cargo on the deck of a heaving aircraft carrier, and Katy felt threatened by it.

She had to change her mindset. Rather than focus on the task and the outcome (failure . . . shame), she intentionally worked on redirecting her thinking. It was about the process of flying the helicopter and all of the preparation before and after the flight. "Just keep doing it, you will get better, you will get there," she remembers telling herself. And she did, going on to a military career that involved landing lots of cargo on lots of ships.

Having the right mindset is the foundation upon which all other aspects of Learned Excellence are built. It is the operating system to the mental software that differentiates top performers from the rest. Katy didn't set out on her path to success until she changed mentally. "I learned to enjoy the roller coaster along the way," Katy says. "Now, when things go wrong I'm always sure to ask myself the question, what is there to learn from this? The ability to ask ourselves that question and to truly sit in the pain of the rejection or setback allows us to grow. Every setback, failure, or rejection has yielded different answers to the question."

This is true of every top performer I have interviewed or worked with. At some point in their lives they absorbed lessons that helped them shift their mindset, to the extent that they all exhibit a remarkably consistent set of characteristics. The best performers are not complacent ("complacency is the enemy"). They constantly look for an advantage. They are humble. They are tenacious. They seek to be part of something bigger than themselves. They are driven by potential, and never want to look back on their lives with regret for the things they didn't do. They might enjoy material things, but that's not what drives them; they are more interested in accomplishing a mission or vision. These are the traits of a high-performance mindset, the traits that Katy, despite a remarkable record of success, had to build within herself.

WHAT IS MINDSET?

The term *mindset* is a relatively modern one. Scarcely seen in books before the mid-1970s, its usage has jumped more than a thousandfold since then.[1] Similarly, appearances of *mindset* in Google searches have gone up more than tenfold since 2004, no doubt pushed by the publication in 2006 of Carol Dweck's book *Mindset: The New Psychology of Success*.[2] So *mindset* has gone from obscure to common over the past couple of decades; today we all hear and talk about it frequently. But what does it mean?

There's no formal definition of *mindset* in the American Psychological Association's dictionary, but there is one for the German word *bewußtseinslage*, which denotes "mental experiences or activities that cannot readily be analyzed into a chain of associations based on images or sensations." This term was first coined by a set of German psychologists working in the early twentieth century who found that becoming intensely involved in a particular task activates the "cognitive procedures" needed to complete the task. They called this phenomenon bewußtseinslage (English translation: state of consciousness, or that which is achieved when listening to Pink Floyd's *The Dark Side of the Moon* at night, under the stars, using your best earbuds). They associated higher bewußtseinslage with better performance, so they were the first psychologists to posit that how one approaches a task mentally—their mindset, in today's vernacular—activates "cognitive procedures" that lead to better outcomes.[3]

More recently, psychologists who couldn't pronounce *bewußtseinslage* (or didn't have *ß* on their keyboards) started using *mindset* instead, and came up with descriptions somewhat more relatable than their German predecessors. Stanford professor Carol Dweck defines mindset as "a mental frame or lens that selectively organizes and encodes information, thereby orienting an individual toward a unique way of understanding an experience and guiding one toward corresponding actions and responses." According to Dweck, having a mindset is necessitated by our world of complex and often conflicting information. It is a "simplifying system" that helps us organize and make sense of the world.[4]

OK, maybe not all that relatable. Another Stanford psychologist, Alia Crum, did a bit better when she defined mindset as "core assumptions that we have about domains or categories of things that orient us to a particular set of expectations, explanations, and goals. . . . Mindsets are ways of viewing reality that shape what we expect, what we understand, and what we wanna do."[5]

Or, let's go with my definition: mindset is how one sets their mind to face every situation.

Regardless of the precise definition, virtually all psychologists agree on one point: mindset is powerful. We know from years of medical research that what the mind believes directly affects the body. It's called the placebo effect: a positive outcome resulting from the *belief* that a beneficial treatment has been received, whether or not it actually has. This is why medical research must always test the performance of the drug or treatment alongside the performance of a fake drug or treatment (the placebo). That is the only way to ensure that the effect of the treatment isn't just based on the patient's belief in it.

Ample evidence suggests/shows that the placebo effect applies to performance as well. One meta-analysis of twelve studies looked at the effect of giving placebos to competitors in sports ranging from biking to weight lifting. These athletes were told they were being given an "ergogenic aid," which is fancy-speak for a pill that helps improve performance (such as steroids). In every study, all but one of which were published post-2000, athletes received a statistically significant performance boost from the placebo. The improvements ranged up to 50 percent, but most fell between 1 percent and 5 percent. Enough to make a difference at the high end of any competition.

The study finds that "the logical conclusion from any study in which an athlete performs to a higher level as the result of receiving a sham treatment is that there is untapped psychological potential in that athlete. Whatever the mechanisms underlying placebo effects in sport, it certainly seems incumbent on sports scientists to further investigate the potential for placebo effects to enhance performance."[6] If a placebo can unlock at least a few percentage points of upside, then perhaps mental performance techniques can as well.

Superstitions, which are plentiful among athletes and many

other performers, are a form of placebo and have a similar positive effect. One study, published in 2010, showed that competitors across a range of contests (golf, memory, puzzles) who used some form of good-luck charm (crossing fingers, wearing a lucky piece of clothing or jewelry) performed materially better than the nonsuperstitious control group. Digging deeper, the psychologists learned that one factor to that improved performance is "task persistence." People empowered by a superstitious belief are more confident they will succeed, so when faced with challenges they persist more. Because if you've got your lucky penny in your pocket, why would you stop trying?[7]

These placebo effects simply mean that what we believe affects how we perform. If we believe we have ingested a pill that will make us perform better, we will perform better, regardless of what's actually in the pill. If we believe that a lucky object or saying will help us perform better, it will. These tricks help tap that untapped potential, but they don't have to be tricks. Mindset is a choice.

Most people wake up every day with the mindset they have always had. It is the mindset that evolved out of their experiences, environment, personality, demographics, intellect, upbringing, genetics, and other factors. It is not a mindset they intentionally chose and shaped; rather it is the one bestowed upon them. The way most people set their mind to take on the ups and downs of life is not deliberate, it is by default. This isn't quite as bad as setting out to summit a mountain by tying on a blindfold and spinning ten times, but it's not far off.

Many of the performers I know started out with their default mindset and got far with it. But none of them got to be the very best that way. Like Katy, they hit a proverbial wall. At that point they made a conscious decision to change their mindset. How to do this is what the rest of this chapter is about:

- Choose your mindset.
- Practice and improve it.
- Learn how to adjust it based on your role.

Get this right, make it a habit, and it's like taking one of those placebo pills every day.

CHOOSE YOUR MINDSET

You've likely heard of pickleball, a game that's sort of like tennis but played on a smaller court with a plastic ball and an oversize Ping-Pong paddle. Invented in 1965,[8] it has recently grown in popularity (by some accounts, the fastest-growing sport in the world) because it's fun, easy to learn, and just about anyone can play. Many people treat it as more of a social engagement than a competitive sport. Sure, they keep score, but the true intent is to chat it up with the couple on the other side of the net.

Not me. When it comes to pickleball, I'm competitive as hell. My wife, Andrea, and I used to play doubles frequently, and I would always look for weaknesses in my opponents and do my best to exploit them. When we were close to winning, I upped my game. That is why I said "used to": she will rarely play doubles with me now, because I get too competitive and detract from what most of the other doubles teams are after, a social and fun afternoon. I developed these competitive traits through years of playing tennis in my younger days. I used to watch how the more experienced guys who beat me approached the game mentally and did my best to emulate them. Now I automatically adopt that mindset whenever I step on a court, pickle or otherwise.[9]

But, in my role as a clinical and performance psychologist, I listen and I'm empathetic. I may look for weaknesses, but for the purpose of helping my client, not to beat them. I'm persistent and tenacious, but not competitive; winning isn't the point. Different role, different mindset required for success.

NBA basketball star Stephen Curry is quoted as saying, "Success is not an accident. Success is actually a choice." To which I would add, so is mindset. (Then I would say, "And keep hitting those threes, Steph," and he would smile and give me a high five.) You can go with your default, or you can choose the mindset required to be the best. To do that, first you need to know where you are going. Think about the roles you have in your life. You are a student, an employee, a manager and leader, an entrepreneur. You are a parent, a sibling, a son or daughter. You may be a spouse or partner. You are a friend. You are a member of communities, be it a team, a troupe, a school, a nonprofit, a union, a club. You have many roles, and excellence in each of those roles requires a certain mindset.

To choose your mindset, first pick one of your roles—the one where you are a performer. For most of us, that's our job or profession. Write down the top traits you think are required for success. *"To be a successful _____, I need to be (more) _____."* These may be things you have observed firsthand from watching and talking to others, or picked up in articles, blogs, or books by and about the best performers in your field. For example, the mindset traits of a successful teacher (patient, strict, listening, commanding, empathetic, flexible, forgiving) are very different from those of a prosecutor (stern, tough, unforgiving, competitive, pragmatic, relentless, ready to exploit any weakness).

As you go through this process and are writing down those traits to which you aspire for each role, it may feel similar to the values process we went through in the last chapter. But while values are inward facing, capturing and codifying the things we care about most deeply, mindset traits are outward facing. What are the personality characteristics we want to bring to bear on each of our roles? For the most part we don't want to change our values, we want to understand them. But mindset traits, those are changeable. If reaching our fullest potential requires a different mindset, we can make that happen.

As I noted earlier, most of the top performers I have worked with share a common set of mindset traits. These may become part of the lists you create: noncomplacent; always looking for an edge; humble; tenacious; want to be part of something bigger; driven by mission, not material gains. Above all else, they universally possess a "growth mindset." This is a term coined and popularized by Dr. Carol Dweck, who defines it as:

> Individuals who believe their talents can be developed (through hard work, good strategies, and input from others) have a growth mindset. Those who believe their talents are innate gifts possess a more fixed mindset. People with growth mindsets tend to achieve more than those with fixed mindsets because they worry less about looking smart and invest more energy into learning.[10]

We are all born curious, wired to seek out challenges and opportunities to learn. This is why toddlers approach strangers, dogs, and ice cream with eyes wide open. They drop things just to see what happens (doesn't that sound like fun?). A wealth of research backs this up, including recent studies that show that children take on such "exploration" even when they understand the potential costs (that is, failure) at stake.[11]

Most of us lose that natural growth mindset as we age into puberty and young adulthood. But not everybody. In findings that reverberated with eager parents everywhere, Dweck and team's research shows that children who receive a higher proportion of "process praise" from their parents as toddlers are bound for greater academic success several years on, and that success is derived primarily from their growth mindset. If a parent praises your effort and approach on something ("I love how you kept trying!"), you are better set up for success than if they praise the outcome or person ("Nice painting, aren't you a great artist!"). Why does this "process praise" lead to success? Because it instills in kids the belief that intelligence and other skills are malleable. They can be improved through effort and process. This in turn gives them more confidence to take on challenges, helping them build those skills. It's a self-fulfilling, virtuous cycle. If you've noticed a change in discourse at your neighborhood playground over the years, this is why.[12]

When the foundation of your thinking (your "implicit theory") is that your mental abilities are fixed, then that shall be so. You will not learn or grow. But if your implicit theory is that your intellect and personality are dynamic, then that shall also be so. Challenges and failures are a starting point to learn more, to get better, to try again.

A complementary bookend to a growth mindset is the concept of grit, which has been popularized by University of Pennsylvania professor Angela Duckworth and her 2016 book, *Grit: The Power and Passion of Perseverance*. While growth mindset is the belief that ability is malleable, not fixed, grit is the tendency to pursue long-term goals with steadfast dedication. Duckworth breaks this down into two primary components, effort (persevering) and passion (maintaining interest), both applied over a long-term time frame. Grit and growth are distinct mindsets—one can have grit without growth, and vice versa—but they also reinforce each other. A 2020 study coauthored by Duckworth found that "adolescents who believed that intellectual ability is malleable [growth mindset] subsequently worked steadfastly toward challenging goals even after accounting for their prior beliefs. To an even greater degree, the converse was also true; higher measured grit predicted subsequent rank-order increases in growth mindset." If you have grit, you are more likely to develop a growth mindset and vice versa.[13]

There are other powerful mindset descriptors besides "growth." Optimism is a big one. It's often related to growth (it's darn hard to be a pessimist and maintain a growth mindset) and is also self-fulfilling. People are more likely to take on challenges and persist in working toward a goal if they believe they are likely to succeed. Warrior mindset is also something I hear a lot. It refers, among other things, to the tenacity and commitment to complete a task no matter how challenging. Ambitious is another trait to consider, as research shows that it is directly correlated with success (happiness may be another story!).

One last point on choosing your mindset traits: keep balance in mind. The mindset descriptors that you choose (tenacious! optimistic!) will most likely be positive; I have yet to meet someone who aspires to sloth and corruption. But there can be too much of a good thing. Optimism is great, but come to rely too much on it and you will become complacent: "I don't need to work at this, everything will turn out great!" This so-called "inverted U" effect is described by Adam Grant and Barry Schwartz as when "positive phenomena reach inflection points at which their effects turn negative." They cite Greek philosopher Aristotle, who posited that to achieve happiness and success, people should cultivate virtues at mean or intermediate levels between deficiencies and excesses."[14] (Rather than Aristotle's "golden mean," they might have gone with Goldilocks and her "just right" mantra, but Aristotle is much more intellectual.)

This is why you need to have mindset traits that balance. Confidence balances with humility. Hard work balances with . . . balance, giving yourself time to relax and recharge. Self-efficacy (belief in one's ability to perform) balances with a desire for constant improvement. As you choose descriptors for your aspirational mindset, keep these balances in mind.

STAY IN THE CIRCLE

Now you have collected a set of awesome traits that describe your desired mindset. But, so what? Those are just words on a page or screen. We may want to be growth and challenge-oriented, ambitious, tenacious, humble, ass kickers. The hard part is, how to get there? Very few people are innately blessed with the mindset that's ideal for their field. We would all love to be Dweckian growers and Duckworthian gritters, but most of us have a lot of Charlie Brown in us, too. How do you *practice* the mindset you've chosen? How do you make it part of your everyday life?

My answer: the controllables. Among all the top performers I have worked with or interviewed, the ones at the top will talk about controlling what they can control and not worrying about the rest. This is a skill that is difficult to master, but in my experience it is through the controllables that one can best evolve into and practice a mindset.

Controllables are simply the things within your control. You can't control whether or not it's going to rain; you can control if you bring an umbrella. There is attitude: the way you think about a thing or person. There is effort: how hard you work. And there is behavior: the actions you take. That's it, that's all you can control: your attitude, your effort, and your behavior. The rest, ignore. As Greek philosopher Epictetus noted, "There is only one way to happiness and that is to cease worrying about things which are beyond the power of our will." Or, if you prefer your philosophers younger and wiser, listen to Linus from *Peanuts* when he says "learning to ignore things is one of the great paths to inner peace."

I debate with myself whether or not a focus on controllables is an attribute of mindset or a framework to bring mindset to life. My conclusion is that it doesn't matter; those are semantics. What does matter is the mantra "attitude, effort, *and* behavior." To live your mindset you need to activate it through all three controllables simultaneously; two or one out of three won't cut it. For example, let's say one of your chosen mindset traits is tenacity. Great! Now what? Well, suppose you are faced with a challenging situation.

How are you going to act? Your attitude will be to stay positive and keep trying until you get it right; you're tenacious, remember? Your effort will be high, because tenacious people work harder in the face of failure. Finally, your behavior will be to try different strategies and tactics, because tenacious people don't just keep doing the same thing over and over—they adjust. Now you have taken that word on a page, *tenacity*, and brought it to life via attitude, effort, and behavior. The word is cool, it looks good on a resume. The attitude, effort, and behavior, though, are how stuff gets done.

The best performers become very good at controlling the controllables and ignoring the rest, but that can be challenging. It helps to have a mantra, so I encourage my clients to "stay in the circle." What's in the circle? Attitude, effort, and behavior: the stuff you can control. What's outside the circle? Everything else, all the stuff you can't control. When my clients start to worry about that stuff—what other people are saying, thinking, or doing, or what the conditions might be—I always remind them to stay in the circle. Soon they start saying it to themselves.

For many performers, the stuff outside the circle includes mostly mundane things like poor weather conditions, negative reviews and comments, and tough competition. But it can also include more profound issues, such as a bad financial or family situation. These may be uncontrollable, but are also practically impossible to ignore. Nevertheless, successful outcomes lie in narrowing your thoughts to just the controllables, and, for a while at least, ignoring the other stuff. Mantras such as "stay in the circle" are helpful, as they are a reminder to redirect and focus attention on attitude, effort, and behavior, away from outside circumstances and the daunting challenges they may entail.

PRACTICE ATTITUDE

Dave Wurtzel spent nearly two decades as a firefighter before turning his attention to his nonprofit The First Twenty, which builds and delivers holistic fitness and performance programs for firefighters and first responders throughout the country. (I got to know Dave when he contacted me after hearing me on a podcast.)

Along with his day job of putting out fires, Dave was a two-time champion in the Firefighter Combat Challenge World Championships. The Firefighter Combat Challenge (now called the Firefighter Challenge) started in 1974 as a research project to set fitness standards for firefighters. The researchers developed a series of five common or critical firefighting tasks—the high-rise pack carry, hose hoist, forcible entry, hose advance, and victim rescue. Participants, selected from various fire departments, geared up for and ran through a timed course, executing the tasks one after the other. When the results were analyzed, it became clear that fitness was directly correlated with higher performance.

One of the lead researchers, Dr. Paul Davis, noted that the participants in the study were quite competitive when running through the tasks. It took a while, but in 1991 Dr. Davis organized the first Firefighter Combat Challenge, with fire departments from around Washington, DC, participating. A couple of years later, ESPN started to carry the events, tagging them as "the toughest two minutes in sports," since completing the five-task obstacle course usually took about two minutes. For elite competitors, not you or me.

Dave Wurtzel was part of the winning relay team in the over-fifty division at the Firefighter Combat Challenge World Championships in 2017 and 2018. So he was brimming with confidence as he and his teammates approached the 2019 finals in Montgomery, Alabama. "We went out to practice it a few times, and we were so confident, we got this!" he recalls. "I came out for the first run and I'm killing it. Then I fell. I was running through the slalom section, and I tripped and fell."

That's when the negative self-talk started. "My mind became focused on this one thing, the fall. That's all I could think about. We were staying at a hotel across the street from the course, and I'd wake up at four a.m. and look out the window at the course, at the spot where I had fallen, and all I could think about was falling. I had run that course over a hundred times successfully, but all I could think about was the one time I failed.

"My brain was doing me in. I would try to tell myself I need to perform, but my brain would respond, *Yeah but you fell*. I need to perform. *Yeah but you fell*. It's like I was having an argument with myself." Dave won that argument. It took some focused work, but he gradually replaced that negative self-talk with positive self-talk. He told himself about how he would run the course and do it right, and it worked. His team came in second, and he didn't fall again.

We already know that talk influences mindset. Parents who praise effort engender a growth mindset in their children; peers who taunt about failures lead to a fixed one. The same is true of self-talk, the internal voice that gives words to feelings and perceptions. Self-talk is how our belief system talks to us, and our belief system controls how we react and respond to most situations. This can be good or bad. If your self-talk is positive (*you'll get them next time*), the consequence resulting from a negative experience is likely to be better than if your self-talk is negative (*man, you suck*). After he fell during that practice run, Dave Wurtzel found himself stuck with the latter. He had to take over that inner voice and redirect it back to positive (*you can do this*) in order to succeed.

The best way to practice the first controllable—attitude—is to manage your self-talk. As you go through your day and encounter various challenges (the conversation that doesn't go your way, the failed opportunity for that glib one-liner, the little mistakes of life), observe what you tell yourself about yourself. Filter out your chatter about others (*That jerk just cut in line!*) and notice your chatter about yourself (*How could I let him do that? That's just like me, being too nice.*) When you talk to yourself, are you a critic or a coach?

Then, practice changing it. Whenever you notice yourself saying something that reflects the attitude you want to improve, make yourself stop. But don't let that internal voice go quiet; rather give it a new mantra to repeat. Change from arguing with that inner voice (*You can do this! No, you can't and you'll look stupid when you fail.*) to having it affirm you (*You can do this, and won't it be fun once you succeed!*) This may sound trite, like cliché-ridden-poster-with-bald-eagle-flying-past-craggy-alpine-peak-backdrop level of trite, but it actually works. You'd be surprised how many top performers are repeating these positive affirmations to themselves as they emerge onto their field, stage, or conference room of performance. Most of them are consciously filling their minds with positive self-talk. "You're ready, you're good, you're prepared, you're relaxed, you can do this. And doggone it, people like you." (OK, maybe not this last one, unless the performer is Al Franken's early-1990s *Saturday Night Live* character Stuart Smalley.)

Many research papers have validated the performance benefits of self-talk. For example, a 2011 meta-study reviewed forty-seven different studies evaluating the effect of self-talk on athletic performance. The scientific conclusion: it works.[15] Other research points out how language matters. For example, a 2016 paper summarizes numerous studies showing how people who reflect on their negative self-talk often end up trying to analyze why they are reacting that way, which can, unfortunately, lead to more negative self-talk.[16] Such rumination is a detriment to performance. This happens because self-reflection usually occurs from a "psychologically immersed" perspective, which makes it challenging to approach the issue objectively or without emotion. The solution is to self-distance, approaching the situation more like a good friend or family member would. This was confirmed by a 2019 study, which showed that competitive cyclists performed better when they used second-person self-talk (*You are a great rider*) instead of first person (*I'm a great rider*).[17]

The corollary to self-talk is just talk, as in what you say to others. Practicing a positive attitude requires aligning your self-talk and external talk around the positive mindset traits you want to practice. While you notice your self-talk, also notice what you are saying to others. The SEALs have a saying, "Calm is contagious." My corollary: emotion is contagious. What you express to others, positive or negative, can shift their mindset and reinforce yours. Just like with self-talk, if you notice yourself using negative language in describing situations to others, practice changing it to positive.

PRACTICE EFFORT

Being a part of the Miami Heat organization isn't for everyone. In case there's any doubt about that, Erik Spoelstra often wears a T-shirt around the office and practice gym that proclaims WE'RE NOT FOR EVERYONE. It's not being arrogant, Erik explains. "Our core values are that we want to be the hardest-working, best-conditioned, most professional team. Every day we are striving to be better. We expect everyone to get on the routine. Hit the weight room, check your weight and body fat every week. Talk to the nutritionist. That turns some players away; they don't want that accountability."

How often do you look back on a performance and think that you could have done better if only you had worked—studied, practiced, iterated, focused—harder? If you are like most people, including most of the high performers I have worked with, the answer is often. And it is almost always true: put in more work, and you will get better and achieve more success.

Effort is perhaps both the easiest and hardest aspect of mindset to practice. Easy because you know what needs to be done: more practicing, more studying, more exercising, more time. Hard because: more work. For some people (and many high performers) hard work is innate. They keep at it naturally; they don't have to make themselves do it. But most of us are what I like to call "human": we have a limit. When we reach that fork in our day when we could spend an hour practicing that thing we care about or rot our brain watching viral videos or reality shows, too often we opt for the videos. We'll practice tomorrow. We suffer from (or benefit from, depending on whether you are sitting comfortably on your couch or not) an intention-behavior gap. We intend to do something, but we don't do it.

When you reach that work-or-relax fork, choose the former. Be aware that the intention-behavior gap yawns before you, and choose to bridge it. Choose effort. Not 100 percent of the time—

that's a path to burnout—but more often than you do now. It helps to score yourself, because you aren't going to jump the couch potato–to–workaholic chasm in one glorious leap. Notice those times in the day when you have a choice of how to spend your next hour, then notice the choices you make on how to use that time. What is your "effort quotient"? Figure out this different version of EQ, then work on improving it. You don't need to get to 100 percent, just a bit better today than you were yesterday. (We'll get into making sure you use that time well in the next chapter.)

Controlling effort isn't just about investing more time; it's about how to invest that time. Remember back to our goals chapter, where Carli Lloyd told us about her lists. That's a good way to get the most out of your invested effort. Part of the effort is to have a plan on how to use that time.

Erik Spoelstra goes all lawyer to bridge the gap. Before every season, he asks his players and coaches to sign written agreements committing to do the work. "You have to commit to a growth mindset," he says. "You have to commit to the sacrifice and effort. To be part of something special and bigger than yourself, there has to be an intention and understanding of what sacrifice means."

PRACTICE BEHAVIOR

The third controllable is behavior: the decisions we make and actions we take that reflect our mindset. Mindset directly influences behavior, but the opposite is also true. For example, most baseball players now have "walk-up songs," a clip of music that gets played on the stadium speakers as the player is walking up to bat. This first started with a Chicago White Sox organist named Nancy Faust in 1970, who started playing different songs for different players. The practice grew after the 1989 movie *Major League*, which featured closer Ricky "Wild Thing" Vaughn, played by Charlie Sheen, coming into a tight game in the ninth inning with the entire stadium rocking to the song "Wild Thing."

The walk-up song is a public example of a performance practice that's been around as long as recorded music: playing a certain song to get ready for a big moment. We all have them, that song we fire up before a big test, interview, or date, to get us psyched up. What all those people rocking to their psych-up song flowing through their earbuds may not realize is that they are codifying their pre-performance routine.

These pre-performance routines are common in the sports world. College basketball coach John Wooden, who won ten NCAA titles while at the University of California, Los Angeles, in the 1960s and '70s, taught his players to put on their socks and tie their shoes the exact same way before every game. This wasn't about the shoes, it was about the routine. By performing the exact same routine before every performance, you are telling your mind and body to get ready, it's almost go time. You are probably doing this without even realizing it: that cup of coffee that you *have to have* in the morning is as much about the routine as it is about the caffeine (right now a lot of you are shaking your heads and saying it's the caffeine!). It's a signal to your mind and body that the day's performance is about to start.[18]

One way to practice mindset is to create a routine that primes your mind to adopt that mindset (or write down the one you already have). It doesn't have to be music; it could involve clothes,

accessories, meals, a mantra, or a moment or minute of meditation. Then, practice the routine, getting the details right every
time. Vary or forget the routine, and you are more likely to settle
into your default mindset rather than your desired one.

Create habits that embody your chosen mindset. Think about
the mindset, observe people who exhibit it, and practice the things
they do that help them live it. Let's say, in your role as a parent, you
want to adopt a mindset of listening more and telling less. Habits
you could adopt to practice this mindset could include putting
your phone far away when you are with the kids. Reflect what you
hear them saying back to them, rather than instantly responding.

How you express yourself, both internally and to others, is a
powerful way to practice mindset. Notice and avoid using language that does not embody your chosen mindset. Develop and
use a mantra that nudges your mind in the right direction, such
as Katy Stanfill's "What is there to learn from this?" Furthermore,
make sure the language you use with others is in sync with what
you are saying to yourself. Misalignment arises when a performer
tells their colleagues positive things (we got this, we can do it)
while their internal self-talk is far less confident. Make it a habit
to listen to the positive things you tell others and use the same
language yourself.

One more way to embody your mindset is to seek out people
with a similar mindset. I often see performers who successfully
practice a high-performance mindset while in their performance
space, but then shift mindsets when they hang out in a different
ecosystem. You might raise your game when hanging out with
other performers, but lower it when around people who have a
different approach. This can drag you down. My parents used to

say, "Tell me who your friends are and I will tell you who you are." I'll add to that: "Tell me their mindset and I'll tell you yours."

PRACTICE FAILURE

Failure is an excellent teacher. Ask Nathan Chen, whose failure at the 2018 Winter Olympics helped him take his mental performance (and subsequent competitive performance) to the next level. Ask Katy Stanfill or Dave Wurtzel, who learned to channel their failures into more positive and successful mindsets.

Or ask Carli Lloyd, one of the best US women to ever play soccer. The 2011 Women's World Cup final was played between the US and Japan in Frankfurt, Germany. The match finished in a 2–2 tie, meaning the World Cup winner would be decided by a penalty kick shoot-out. In the first round of kicks, US midfielder Shannon Boxx missed her kick while Japanese forward Aya Miyama nailed hers. That brought up Carli.

"As I placed the ball down, I started doubting how I wanted to take the penalty, going back and forth in my mind and asking myself should I stick with the same side and pace as my last kick [which she made in the previous match against Brazil]? Or do I change my spot? I said to myself, just hit it with pace. Then I stepped up, kicked the ball, and I missed. It sailed way over the bar. We lost the shoot-out. I was devastated. I felt like I let my teammates and country down. I sulked for a long time after that."

When she stopped sulking, she decided (attitude) that she would never miss another penalty kick (PK) in the World Cup again. She refined her technique (behavior), and practiced it over and over (effort) until it was completely automatic. By the time the 2015 Cup rolled around, Carli was ready. She nailed a PK in a knockout match against Colombia, hitting it to the keeper's left, and had a higher-pressure try in the semifinal against Germany. When the time came to take the PK against Germany, Carli placed the ball on its spot. "I decided after the Colombia game that if I had another PK try I would go to the same side," she says. "There was lots of commotion behind me, but you can see on the video how focused I was. Nothing around me entered my mental space. I stepped up, went to the same side, and put it in the back of the net." The US won the game, advanced to the final, and won the World Cup. "Everyone can hit a PK," Carli tells me. "It's not that difficult. It's about what you tell your mind. If your mind has even one or two percent doubt, it will throw you off. I wasn't prepared in 2011. I was in 2015."

Success is a lousy teacher; failure is a great one. You can draw a straight line from Carli's failure in 2011 to her success in 2015. Just like Nathan, Katy, Dave, and just about every top performer I have ever worked with, they fail, and they learn from those failures to get better.

The problem is, it's no fun to fail. There's a reason it's called the comfort zone: it's comfortable! And safe: no one is going to excoriate you for screwing up when you stay in the comfort zone. This is exactly what your primitive brain craves. It's a product of ancestors who survived numerous life-threatening calamities, so being comfortable and safe is exactly what the doctor ordered.

The comfort zone is why Dave Wurtzel, future Philadelphia firefighter and Firefighter Combat world champion, didn't go out for his eighth-grade basketball team. "I got nervous when I walked out of the locker room, so I never even made it to the court. I never tried. I told my dad that they cut me, and he didn't understand how that could happen on the first day of practice." Apparently Dave didn't learn his lesson, because several years later, when he was a student at Penn State, he once again didn't push himself outside his comfort zone. "There was a girl I had a crush on starting almost the beginning of freshman year. When we were about to graduate, I saw her at an event and I finally got up the nerve to tell her how beautiful she was. She replied, 'I wish you had told me that four years ago!' Then she turned and walked away!"

Dave is a happily married family man now, so he tells this story with a smile and no regret (OK, maybe a tinge of regret). "I never stepped up to the plate. I was afraid of the pressure, I didn't want to fail. It's like that [Wayne] Gretzky quote, you miss one hundred percent of the shots you don't take. I didn't take the shot."

Most people don't take that shot. Some regret it, and some don't even think about it, ensconced as they are in their comfort zone. Unfortunately, staying comfortable is the absolute worst way to practice mindset. Failure teaches us and breeds success, and how we handle it is a defining characteristic of our mindset. That means that to learn excellence you need to practice failure. Deliberately take more risks, leave that comfort zone behind.

Have someone you like, in that tingly not-friend-zone way? Talk to them. A new opportunity comes your way? Say yes. A request for volunteers? Raise your hand. See a flier for an interesting class or club? Sign up. Talk yourself out of things? Talk yourself back in. Performers have the luxury of having many opportunities to fail, so they have ample opportunity to learn from it. But for many of us, performance challenges are more rare, so we have fewer opportunities to fail and learn.

Start in more low-stakes environments. Take on a new game, sport, or pastime, and spend enough time at it to fail a lot. You want to quit, right? Don't! That music your kids are listening to and you can't stand? A great opportunity to practice this! Dance hip-hop! Or try a new type of food you have never had before and would normally never try. Then, if you hate it (failure), take time to learn from the experience, maybe appreciate parts of it (attitude), and see if you can change your mindset and try again (effort). You may spit it out (behavior!) but at least you tried.

The more you fail, the more you get to practice how you respond to failing. As retired SEAL Marcus Luttrell says, "If you don't go out and try to find stress, it will show up for you. Life will find you. If you aren't prepared for something like that, you will get squashed. The first three years of SEAL training, I felt like I failed everything, but I didn't take it personally. Your attitude has to be, it's over the minute it happens. Your attitude has to be, I got this now. I'm not going to fail it twice!" Fail enough and you learn that failure leads to success.

Deliberately practicing failure not only helps develop a growth mindset; it can also spark creativity. Ben Potvin is a former Canadian national gymnast who parlayed his athletic skills into a long career as a performer, head coach, and creative director for Cirque du Soleil, the amazing entertainment company. He sees failure as a "candy store that sparks imagination and creativity." I met Ben in 2015. We worked together at many Performing Under Pressure Camps for elite athletes. Andy Walshe recruited Ben, myself, and many other instructor types to design physical, emotional, and psychological challenges for elite athletes and corporate executives to experience within the camps.

Given Ben's history, first as an acrobat and then as a trainer and creative director for thousands of Cirque du Soleil shows, he became one of the world's best at helping people push beyond what they thought were their human limits. If you've ever been to a Cirque show, you've witnessed repeated physical and creative maneuvers that probably made you shake your head in disbelief and awe. Ben believes these moves were initiated from a place of discomfort. Incremental discomfort creates room for growth. He talks about the relationship between balance and imbalance (what I call comfort and discomfort) as being critical to creativity. "If you want to grow creatively you can't be balanced. You need to get off balance to find new creativity. Challenge yourself. Force yourself to explore something new. Try it and force yourself to either like it or dislike it. Create a spark, then find what you like and get better at it."

Jimmy Lindell spent most of his years in the Navy SEALs as a sniper. He was involved in many engagements, including being part of the team that freed merchant captain Richard Phillips after he was kidnapped by the Somali pirates who hijacked his container ship, the *Maersk Alabama*, in April 2009. (The 2013 film *Captain Phillips* was based on this event.) Before joining the SEALs, Jimmy ran a successful carpet and flooring business, but he took a big step out of that comfort zone when he sold the company to pursue a naval career.

But this isn't an anecdote about shooting or carpeting or the rigors of BUD/S training. It's an anecdote about challenging the comfort zone. "I'm trying to work out of my comfort zone all the time. When I was in the SEALs, I would practice shooting left-handed," the right-handed Jimmy tells me. "Even today, I can't sit back and chill like a man my age should probably do. I can't stay comfortable, I won't." How does a former SEAL Team leader get out of his comfort zone? He sings.

"The other day, I'm driving and this Styx song comes on," Jimmy says. (Styx is a 1970s and '80s rock band.) "I can't sing at all, but I really wanted to try singing this one. So I pulled over to give it my full attention. I even filmed it on my phone. I was so bad, it was hilarious. I showed it to my wife, and she laughed so hard." That's how easy it can be to get out of your comfort zone. Crank the Styx (I recommend their ballad "Come Sail Away," appropriate for a former Navy commander), shoot a video of you singing your heart out, and show it to someone you love.

DON'T SCREAM OVER SPILLED MILK

In 2010, I was the lead psychologist for the West Coast US Navy SEAL Teams (Teams 1, 3, 5, and 7). One morning, a SEAL sniper chief came and knocked on my door. (Chief is the third-highest senior enlisted rank in the Navy, just below senior chief and master chief. Chiefs are critical to success; many officers will tell you they run the Navy.) He had just returned a week earlier from a six-month, highly "kinetic" deployment (meaning lots of enemy engagement), and had run into some trouble at home. His three-year-old kept knocking over his glass of milk at the family dinner table. The boy wasn't doing it on purpose! Nevertheless, by about the fourth or fifth time this happened, the SEAL sniper stood up at the dinner table and screamed at his son, "Stop spilling the milk!"

The boy, scared to death, burst into tears. His mother ordered her husband, the contrite man at my door, to come see me first thing the next morning.

When a SEAL chief is on deployment he expects perfection, both in himself and his team. He demands accountability, vigilance, and full attention to detail. Anything less than that is a potentially dangerous failure. When a father of a three-year-old sits down for dinner, he may secretly wish for perfection, but it's not gonna happen. Milk gets spilled, peas get stuffed up nostrils, spaghetti ends up on the floor; the plate as a place where food resides is merely a concept. Fortunately, these transgressions are messy but not dangerous. Unfortunately, applying the mindset of the sniper chief to the situation of the toddler dad leads to shouting and crying and morning visits with Dr. Potterat. The traits and expectations that are effective in one role are not effective in the other.

More recently I started working with a marketing executive from a well-known clothing and apparel brand. She was juggling roles with which many readers may be familiar: leader of a large team at her company, mother of two, wife of fifteen years, and avid member of a regular golf group. In her job as a marketer, her mindset was all about how people perceived their company's brands, and what she and her team could do to enhance that perception. Then she'd go home and apply the same mindset to her family and friends.

"I just can't stop my branding and marketing mode," she told me a few months after we started working together. "I want to always make sure that our family and my kids look like they represent the family brand well." Her golf friends were getting similar treatment, and were getting fed up with how she constantly talked to them about their brand as golfers, mothers, and women and how they needed to think more about that brand. As our sessions progressed, she reported growing tension with her husband and kids. She and her husband were fighting more, in part due to his frustration with the pressure of maintaining the family "brand" to the world. An engineer, he didn't care that much about what others thought.

Let's say you are a skier. You love nothing more than cruising down snowy hills, carving turns and feeling the cold wind on your face. In your closet you have all the gear: skis, poles, winter clothes, and a big clunky pair of ski boots. Now, let's say a friend of yours invites you to go play basketball. Would you show up wearing those ski boots? Of course not! Ski boots are completely wrong for playing basketball (or anything besides skiing).

Get it? The sport is your role, the gear is your mindset. To be excellent in each one of your roles, you need to choose different mindsets for those roles and deliberately transition between them when you transition between roles. You need to kick off the ski boots and throw on the sneakers. Neither the SEAL sniper chief nor the marketing executive knew how to shift their workplace mindsets to their home roles. They were wearing ski boots to a hoops game.

After the SEAL told me his spilled-milk story that morning, we decided to come up with a ritual to help him shift his mindset when he was home; he didn't want to yell at his son anymore. I asked him if he brushed his teeth every morning. Yes. Then starting tomorrow morning, I suggested, he should look in the mirror while he was brushing and say out loud, "I'm not at training. I'm not deployed. My son is three years old and he is going to spill his milk today. Twice."

The next morning the chief called me to report that while the milk flowed again the previous evening, he had remained calm. "I expected him to do it twice, but it never happened." About a week later, the chief stopped by my office with a bottle of whiskey as a gift and said, "Doc, you're not going to believe this: our son hasn't spilled any milk since that first time after I did the brushing-my-teeth thing. I've been expecting it to happen twice a day, and it hasn't happened at all." (I resisted the urge to spill the whiskey just to see what would happen.)

I also introduced the concept of having different mindsets for different roles to the marketing executive. I asked her to choose a few words that she thought she needed to be successful within each of her roles—her aspirational mindset traits. For her role as a mother, she wanted to be a good listener and guide, patient, loving, and supportive. As a wife, she chose respect, communication, partnership, compromise, and love. For her golf buddies, she came up with fun, exercise, and social connection. And for her career as a marketing and branding executive, she selected detail-oriented, customer-pleasing, and consistent.

Next, we worked on her transition routines. She wrote her roles and words into an app on her phone and made it a habit to read them after leaving work or before stepping onto the golf course. This helped her remind herself of the different mindsets she had chosen for each role. She reported a positive effect almost immediately. She felt like she was more present, happy, and successful in each of her roles, and in retrospect realized how much she had allowed her work mindset to bleed into her personal life. The clothing expert realized that mindsets are a bit like outfits: they can be chosen for different occasions. A few months later I received a very gracious note from her husband, thanking me for saving their marriage! A bold and probably exaggerated claim, but it provides testament to the power of shifting mindsets across roles.

Earlier, we talked about pre-performance routines such as the baseball player's walk-up song as a way to kick-start the performance mindset. When considering role shifts, the post-performance routine is just as important. This is akin to an "off-ramp" for your performance, like a dimmer switch for the bright light that is your performance self. You may play one sort of music and take one route as you commute to work, and another type of music and another route on your way home. These routines are actually training your mind to get into the right mindset. It doesn't matter what your "transition" routine is; what matters is that you have one. You probably already are doing this, so take some time to notice what you do, then codify it by writing it down and make it your habit. Every time you move into that mindset, or move out of it, employ the exact same routine. The technical term for these routines is "boundary-crossing activities," where one enters and exits roles by crossing the boundaries (physical, emotional, temporal) between them.

Retired Navy SEAL Marcus Luttrell tells me a great story of mindset shift. One day he walked into the office of one of his instructors. As Marcus tells it, "This guy was the meanest instructor I ever had the pleasure of meeting. The toughest, fastest, strongest; boy could he yell at you." That day, when Marcus walked into the office, the mean tough guy was cooing into the phone, saying, "Now sweetheart, I'll read you the story when I get home, I promise. I love you."

When he saw Marcus, he instantly switched mindsets. "He always had these sunglasses on," Marcus recalls. "When he saw me, he hung up the phone, nodded his head so that the sunglasses dropped perfectly into place, then proceeded to cuss me out like I had never been cussed out before!" Sometimes a transition routine can be as simple as donning a cool pair of shades.

PATRIOTS VS. FALCONS

The sports landscape is full of amazing comebacks, but few are more remarkable than Super Bowl 51 ("LI" in NFL-speak), played between the New England Patriots and Atlanta Falcons on February 5, 2017, in Houston. The Falcons led the game 28–3 with just over two minutes left in the third quarter, which is when the comeback began. The Patriots scored a touchdown near the end of the quarter, rattled off nineteen straight points in the fourth quarter, and finished the biggest Super Bowl comeback in NFL history with a touchdown in overtime.

There were numerous factors behind the Patriots' remarkable comeback and Falcons' astonishing collapse: skill, luck, fatigue, stress, coaching, play-calling, the refs, and so on. But one potential factor was neither acknowledged nor even recognized by the players or coaches in the swirl following the game: loss aversion. This is the innate human bias toward playing to not lose rather than playing to win when holding the lead. As we get closer to winning, we start to worry more about losing.

A 2011 Wharton School study reviewed the performance of PGA (Professional Golfers' Association) golfers, the best in the world at what is perhaps the most mentally challenging of all sports. They discovered that, controlling for all other factors, professional golfers hit eagle or birdie putts less accurately than they hit similar par, bogie, or double-bogie putts.[19] (An eagle is two under par and a birdie is one under; both are good outcomes. A bogie is one over par, a double bogie two over; both are poor outcomes for a top-level player.) This is loss aversion at work. When given the chance to "win" a hole by scoring a birdie or better, the data shows that players become slightly less aggressive. They don't hit the ball quite as hard, because they want to leave themselves an easier follow-on shot for par. Rather than go for the win, they ease up just a bit to ensure they won't lose. As the study notes, "players invest more focus when putting for par to avoid encoding a loss."[20]

Another study confirms such loss-aversive behavior. In reviewing data on holes that were changed from par 5 to par 4 without a material change in the physical nature of the hole, data shows PGA golfers scored lower when the holes were rated as a par 4 than when the same holes are par 5. This suggests the players try harder when playing to avoid a bogie or worse than when they are playing to maintain their score. For example, a player with an opportunity to putt for a score of 4 will be a tad more aggressive if the hole is a par 4 than when it's a par 5. When it's a par 5, even if they miss the putt they can still get a par. Performance on a particular hole doesn't matter that much, as tournaments are won based on who has the lowest total score at the end of seventy-two holes. Nevertheless, players care about it, at least subconsciously. The researchers calculate this behavior costs players about one stroke over the course of a seventy-two-hole tournament, which, for the top golfers, translates into a loss of $1.2 million in prize money per year![21]

The Wharton golf study notes that its results are consistent with prospect theory, an economic concept developed by psychologists Daniel Kahneman and Amos Tversky in 1979 that predicts people become more risk averse when they are recording gains (putting for birdie or better) than when they are suffering losses (par or worse). Indeed, numerous studies confirm that loss aversion affects performers across a wide variety of fields, from athletics to investing to business. Human thinking is often biased by aversion to loss, so reducing or eliminating the risk of losing becomes more important than increasing the probability of winning. This inherent trait can creep into mindset, with negative effects.

To combat loss aversion, work to maintain mindset throughout a performance. Awareness is a good first step: know what loss aversion is and how this natural bias pushes us to play to not lose rather than win. I urge my clients to continue to focus on the tactics, actions, and behaviors that are leading to success. This is similar to Navy SEALs, who are taught to focus on the mission relentlessly until it is complete. Complacency is the enemy. This is drilled into them until it is second nature and the innate loss aversion bias is obliterated. Keep the foot on the gas pedal until the job is done; don't coast. Playing to win is a cliché, but also an important mindset trait exhibited by every top performer with whom I have worked.

MIND OVER TEMPLE

Mike Dauro grew up on the Gulf Coast of southern Mississippi and moved west when he received an ROTC scholarship at the University of Colorado. While at Boulder he walked on to the toughest team on campus: the "Ralphie Handlers." This is the team of student athletes who manage the university's mascot, a buffalo named Ralphie. They care for her, take her to various events, and, before every home football game, accompany her on a raucous run around the field. Sprinting alongside a galloping buffalo is dangerous, and being on that team set Mike up well to pursue his dream of becoming a Navy SEAL.

It wasn't easy, though. Mike's application to the SEALs was rejected three times before he was finally accepted. When he arrived at BUD/S, his mindset was certain. "I'm going to achieve this," he recalls telling himself. "Once I got in, there was no question I was going to get through the training and into the SEAL community. The quit aspect never entered my mind."

Mike succeeded, graduating from BUD/S and spending the rest of his military career as a SEAL. His biggest learning from that experience? Mindset.

"You can be the most physically fit person, but during BUD/S training your body, your temple, is going to be destroyed," he says. "That beautiful temple you built will be demolished. When that happens you need to depend on what's happening from the neck up. If you observe the training, you will see moments when they are mentally down. That grain of sand will turn into a mountain if they don't intercede immediately. Mind fitness is more important than the temple.

"The ability to persevere in these moments is what we look for in someone who is going to be deployed, because on a mission they are going to face those moments when they need that mindset of never giving in, never letting your teammates down."

Mike has his own version of growth mindset: "There are three things I constantly evaluate. Am I growing myself? Am I growing others? Am I growing the team?" He recalls employing this mindset while on a mission in Afghanistan. He and his team spent nearly a year in an Afghan village, advising villagers and tribes on how they could work better together. This was not a typical combat mission; the SEALs had to work with the locals, understand them, and gain their trust. "Some of my counterparts in other villages didn't like this mission because they didn't see it as a 'SEAL' mission. I had a different mindset: this is our mission and the confines we have to work with. Embrace the circumstances and adapt. I taught this to our platoon and did my best to lead by example. We can make this successful. We can work within the boundaries to make this our SEAL mission."

Mike evolved the growth mindset he learned through his years as a SEAL and running Ralphie to transform his team's approach. "Lots of guys joined for direct action, flying to a mission every night. That's what a SEAL mission is to them. We did some of those missions, but we were the most successful team because we had the mindset of how we can get after this as a SEAL mission. We made it work by adapting our mindset."

LEARNED EXCELLENCE
ACTION PLAN—MINDSET

MINDSET IS A CHOICE. TO CHOOSE AND PRACTICE YOURS:

Observe and select the mindset traits that correlate with success in each of your various roles.

Activate your chosen mindset by staying "in the circle" of the things within your control: attitude, effort, and behavior.

To activate your mindset via attitude, observe and alter how you talk to yourself, deliberately replacing negative, irrational sentiments with positive, rational ones.

To activate your mindset via effort, increase your effort. Track and improve your "effort quotient," how often you choose effort over nonproductive time.

To activate mindset via behavior, adopt practices that help you embody that mindset: pre-performance routines, daily habits, aligned internal and external language, and the company of like-minded individuals.

To practice mindset, step out of your comfort zone and take more risks so you can practice how to handle, learn from, and rebound from failure.

To help switch mindsets when shifting roles, develop and practice a transitional ritual or routine.

When you are closing in on success, remind yourself of the mindset that got you there. Be aware of the human tendency to play to not lose.

CHAPTER 5

Process

The time and intensity that you put into
your work and process is what matters.
You don't have to be as perfect as
you think but the mentality has to be
aggressive.

—Rich Hill, MLB pitcher

As part of their normal training routine, Navy SEALs go through something called Close Quarter Combat (CQC). Just like the name implies, this training simulates what the SEALs might encounter when they enter buildings in hostile territory. It takes place in a big labyrinth, with halls, walls, and rooms laid out in such a way as to simulate homes or offices. During CQC, small teams of SEALs (called a "train" in SEAL parlance) move into buildings and rooms with the goal of clearing out enemies and protecting allies. Cardboard silhouettes representing bad and good guys are placed throughout the "house," giving SEALs the opportunity to make shoot/no shoot decisions under pressure. They are assessed by their instructors and leaders based on their tactics, speed, accuracy, ability to discriminate, communication, and teamwork.

In the years when I was the lead performance psychologist for West Coast SEAL Teams, it was my job to help them with CQC. I observed the exercises from a catwalk overlooking the structure, tracking physiological metrics from each soldier via a handheld tablet. This helped me see how well the methods I had taught them to control their stress responses were working. How were they reacting to live-action situations with real ammo? With that feedback I would later coach them on their arousal control techniques (which we cover in detail in the next chapter). I was dressed in camouflage and Kevlar body armor, and protected by the confidence that the best operators in the world wouldn't accidentally shoot their shrink.

One day back in 2010, a team of special forces soldiers from one of our US allies was conducting their version of CQC in an adjacent section of the CQC building. An hour or so after their training session began, the shooting suddenly stopped, replaced by a lot of shouting. One of their team members ran over to us and asked if our medics could come take a look. Curious, I tagged along. One of their soldiers sat in a chair, fuming and having a heated discussion with his teammates. He didn't seem to be in pain, despite the bullet wound in his leg: an entry wound on his thigh with the exit wound a little lower, by the knee. There wasn't a lot of blood: the bullet entered his skin and followed a somewhat miraculous, subcutaneous path down his leg without hitting any major muscles, veins, or arteries. As bullet wounds go, you could hardly have a cleaner one. Still, it must have hurt.

As it turns out, this highly trained and skilled soldier had accidentally shot himself in the leg while unholstering his weapon. The holster he was using was new, and slightly different from the one he was used to, which is reportedly why he had shot himself. The slight change in equipment collided with hundreds of hours of muscle and pattern memory, and the result was an accidentally pulled trigger. The soldier recovered quickly, having learned a valuable lesson in process and change.

Top performers are efficient and consistent. They follow routines in just about everything related to performance: practice, eating, resting, and relaxing. They focus on preparation and trust and leverage their process to perform. They know their process; they don't just wing it. The most experienced pilots will have a preflight checklist, not just a mental one but an actual written checklist. Processes can be complicated; even the most expert practitioners might skip or flub a step here or there if they don't have things documented.

Top performers are extremely particular about maintaining consistency, and only make changes to their process in a stepwise and thoughtful manner. If they have new equipment, they will practice thoroughly with it prior to important performances, as they want to feel confident with any subtle changes to their flow, routines, and processes prior to "going live" when it matters. The shooting was a visceral example of just how important it is for performers to fully understand the details of any new routine or process change prior to their "live" performance. Whether it's a different slide presentation, a different computer, a different place, a different piece of sporting equipment, or a different holster, any changes to your process without practicing can lead to bad outcomes. Like shooting yourself in the leg.

The most critical processes help top performers manage time, information, and changes (to equipment, technique, design and content, health and fitness, and the process itself). A good process for time management helps people get more out of their twenty-four hours per day than anyone else. An information process helps them prioritize valuable information while filtering out noise. A solid approach to change will help them avoid the mistake of overreacting and making rash decisions. Elite performers evolve their processes deliberately. They manage their time carefully so that they get the most out of their twenty-four hours. They monitor their information input carefully, relying on trusted sources and ignoring the rest, so that they are getting the highest-quality knowledge about themselves and their performance. And they make changes carefully, using data and iteration to evolve into the new state.

Will this work for you? Think about the next vacation you plan on taking. How will you go about planning it? You will likely first do research into where you want to go. What time of year is the best? What will the weather be like? Then, what are the best places to stay? What will I or we do while we are there? You will research, check reviews and articles, compare prices, and winnow your choices down until you have a plan. In other words, you have a thoughtful process to get to an optimum outcome: a nice vacation for yourself and your friends or family. Let's say something comes up at the last minute—an event in another location you might want to attend. Do you drop everything, scrap your plan, and change your destination? Probably not. You may adjust your itinerary, add or subtract a day here or there, but after you have followed a methodical process to create a fantastic trip it would take something major for you to completely scrap it.

Many of the people I have worked with had a better process for planning vacations than for achieving their aspirational career or performance goals. We change this, so that processes for performance become ingrained, with high-quality feedback informing calculated changes. The result is that when we say "trust the process," the performers actually do.

Rich Hill was a self-described "happy-go-lucky kid" when he was the starting pitcher for the Chicago Cubs in game 3 of their 2007 playoff series against the Arizona Diamondbacks. Rich has spent many years as a pitcher, and I was able to get to know and work with him when he was with the Dodgers from 2016 to 2019. When he looks back at that 2007 playoff game, he remembers, "I was just happy to be in the big leagues, and was much too preoccupied with the outcome. I lost sight of the moment, lost sight of what I was doing." Rich only made it to the fourth inning of the game, giving up three runs and taking the loss. The D'Backs swept the series from the Cubs.

Rich attributes that loss to having an outcome-focused mentality rather than a process-oriented one. He started to shift toward process around 2010, well before he met me. "I developed a whole different intensity about me, a focus on the moment, conviction and confidence that it all will come together. I make it as simple as possible." He frequently refers to the moment the ball comes out of his hand. This is what he can control, along with every step of the process leading up to the pitch.

"Everyone has talent, the separator is what you are going to do to get better," says Rich. "The idea is to get one percent better. If you get one percent better at the major-league level, that's a lot. The time and intensity that you put into your work and process is what matters. Younger guys get caught up in being perfect. You don't have to be as perfect as you think but the mentality has to be aggressive."

What would he tell his 2007 self? "Summon up the intensity and courage, and go for it. You can do all the right things and still have a negative outcome. If things don't turn out well it sucks, but it sucks a lot more if you don't go for it."

THE SAME TWENTY-FOUR HOURS

Look at the best performers in the world in any field. What do they have that you don't have? How about amazing physical and intellectual attributes, sharply honed skills, powerful personalities (some good, some not so good), charisma, good looks, fame, and fortune. OK, OK, but what about the stuff that really matters, the most important currency known to mankind? What about time? No difference between them, me, and you. We all have twenty-four hours per day. Now I know this is a cliché: I just typed "you have the same" into Google, and it helpfully completed the sentence by adding "24 hours as Beyoncé." Which is technically true but effectively not. Beyoncé, and other very wealthy people, have plenty of help with daily tasks such as cleaning, cooking, commuting, and flying private jets to St. Barts. So let's amend the statement to "We all have twenty-four hours per day, except Beyoncé and others like her whose money buys them more time." The vast majority of people I work with, from SEALs to athletes to business leaders to first responders, are more like us, the normal people for whom twenty-four hours is really twenty-four hours, than the Beyoncés of the world.

We spend a chunk of those hours sleeping, around eight hours per day if you adhere to most commonly accepted health guidelines. Which leaves us sixteen waking hours per day. (Many people routinely get fewer than eight hours per day of sleep, and a few may even be able to maintain top performance while living with such a chronic deficit, but most people eventually pay a penalty in performance and other important life factors.)

That's your budget: sixteen hours per day. How will you spend it?

One of my first requests when I start working with new clients is for them to share their calendar with me. When they do, I almost always find open spaces in their days, blank slots when nothing is formally scheduled. When I ask about these time slots, the usual response is that it's time used to catch up, or fit in a workout, or talk to family.

How about you? Take a moment right now to open your calendar. Let's look at last week. Pick a day. Is it nicely full of activities or commitments? Or are there blank slots scattered about? If you are like most of my clients when we start working together, the answer is the latter.

Do you have a wallet on you right now? How about you open it up, take out a fistful of cash, and toss it in a garbage can. If you've gone cashless, use your phone to tap a metaphorical payment terminal and send some money—enough to hurt—out into the ether, never to be seen again. That's what you are doing with those blank spaces on your calendar; they are like throwing away time, your most valuable currency. You won't throw fistfuls of bills away, but you'll leave an hour on a Wednesday afternoon completely unscheduled. Of course you'll do *something* during that time, but that something may be dictated by any one of a number of factors: who happens to call you then, which clickbait headline comes across your feed, or which email happens to be at the top of your inbox. This is waiting for life to tell you what's important. That blank space on the calendar gets filled by whatever happens to be top of mind at that moment.

Learning excellence requires getting the very most out of the time you have, which means actively choosing how to use every minute of it. This is a hallmark of every top performer I have worked with: they are very good at managing their time. Despite having more demands than most people, they are better at getting things done across all aspects of their lives. They are a paradox, in that they are both the busiest people and the most effective. Hence the old saying, "If you want something done, give it to a busy person." Why? They manage their time better.

A wide variety of research shows that effective time management also contributes to well-being. A 2017 meta-analysis of such studies concludes that "nonexperimental and experimental findings suggest that time management can improve people's quality of life, lower stress, boost job satisfaction, and enhance other facets of well-being."[1]

Ted Brown, the executive at Lockton, tells me that his calendar is a "critical part of my ability to perform at a high level. Before I leave home in the morning, I know what the day holds. I plan my weeks, months, and years with the same format. There is a rhythm to every week. For example, Mondays are to get my teams and me mobilized. Tuesdays through Thursdays are set up for front-footed movement, and Fridays are to recap and close things out. There is a rhythm to my days, too. I wake up. I meditate for ten minutes. I work out. I come home, make breakfast with my kids, and help get them off to school. I take a shower, turning the water as cold as it goes for five minutes. This stimulates my brain, gets me thinking clearly. I repeat my mantra, which keeps me clear on what I want to be, who I am, who I am serving. My best time for thinking is in the morning, so that's when I schedule client meetings and prep time or leadership initiatives. Lunchtime is a good time to meet with the team, and afternoons are more task oriented."

Ted's calendar reflects his values and the balance for which he strives in his life. It includes space for exercise—"I have to get the beast out physically in order to calm myself mentally"—as well as meditation and family time. He sticks to it: "My routine is sacred. I'm almost maniacal about maintaining it."

Ted's system for time management is one I came up with when I was in the Navy, working with SEALs as well as many top performers on the side. I was driving to work, a little rushed and worried about traffic. Suddenly it dawned on me that all of the top performers I was working with were very good with time management. They got plenty of sleep, but still seemed to have more hours in their day than most people, as if they never ended up sitting in traffic, stressed and anxious. I committed to getting better at using my twenty-four hours, devising my own system. So now, every Sunday evening I break out my calendar and look at the next ten days. I spot the blank spaces and fill them with tasks or activities, the things that I value. I find that ten days is about the right amount of time for planning ahead. I know what my priorities are for the next week and a half, and if I have spare time on my calendar I know how to best fill it. These don't always need to be ambitious—you'll see some "catch up on email" slots on my calendar. The same with time for meditation, thinking, and catching up on administrative tasks or the news. The point is to write these things down and fill your time intentionally; remember that if things are written down they are more likely to get done. Every Sunday, fill the white space by writing stuff down.

But life happens, right? Any calendar system needs to be flexible. I use color coding to help with that. During those Sunday calendar reviews, after I fill the white spaces I go back through every day and make sure all the time slots are color-coded, green, yellow, or red. The green events are most flexible—they can be moved or even canceled if something more important comes up. Yellow events are also flexible, but I only change them if I absolutely have to. And if something is red it is practically sacred, taking precedence over virtually anything else that might come up. Greens are things like administrative stuff, routine meetings, thinking and planning time, or (for me, alas) workouts. For yellow, think routine doctor or dentist appointments, internal meetings, friend lunches. Red might be an anniversary or birthday dinner, client meetings, or cramming to get a critical project done on time. The colors and how you use them are entirely subjective.

I'm sure my system is not revolutionary. There are probably plenty of other ones out there that are just as good. But what's not as good is what so many people do. Maybe Ted Brown is being a tad dramatic when he says "blank space is death"; many people live well into old age with blanks on their calendars. But just a tad:

blank space is a gateway to procrastination or wasted time, which can kill performance.

Right now, many of you are nodding. You're right, Eric, you're saying. I'm going to get right on that calendar thing and wipe out those blank spaces. But others are thinking, I like my blank spaces! They give me time to do stuff, or relax, or screw around. I don't want to fill all that time up. I want to own my calendar; I don't want it to own me.

To which I say, why not? You can still have time to goof off, watch videos, read, or waste time doing something fun and mindless. In fact, you can have more of that time if you are intentional about it. Putting it in your calendar makes it your choice. It also makes sure we remember to do all the things we need to do that we will likely otherwise forget. To help people get over this sentiment, I might start off by having them fill just some of the white space, and leaving some unfilled. Once they see how well this works they often go all in.

The other question people have is how to handle the inevitable things that come up. In the world of computer programming, an interrupt-driven system is one where one component of a system signals another that it needs something to be done, or that it has completed a requested task. The component being signaled may pause what it's doing to act on the request. In essence, one component interrupts the other, making it drop what it was working on and pay attention.

People are interrupt driven, too. We may be working on something but are easily distracted by something—anything—else that comes along. We're like Dug, the talking dog in the movie *Up*, when he sees a squirrel. You are going along doing your thing, when something comes up that interrupts your flow—squirrel! Rather than ignoring the interruption, you make it your priority in the moment.

My color-coding system handles interrupts beautifully, since when you receive them you already have prioritized your time blocks. In the middle of a green appointment? Interruptible. Yellow or red? Probably not, but you can look forward in your day or week to find time that would work. No system is perfect and often you need to make a judgment call. Is the interrupt from your boss worth moving your dentist appointment for? Yes. Is it worth missing your kid's birthday party? Your call, but for me the answer is no. Regardless of how you prioritize things, having an "intentional" calendar gives you a framework to manage the inevitable interrupts, so that you can be in more control of them.

Alex Krongard has a useful metaphor when it comes to prioritizing interrupts. Alex retired from the Navy as a rear admiral, after a thirty-one-year career mostly spent with the SEALs, including stints as the commanding officer of SEAL Team 7 and as a naval staff member on the National Security Council. When we talk about how to manage time, Alex thinks about a boat metaphor he first learned from his father. If there is a hole in the hull, is it above the waterline or below it? If it is above the waterline, the boat is not in immediate danger of sinking. Below the line means time to start bailing. When something comes up for Alex, he uses that test: Is it above or below the waterline? Above means you have the luxury of time. If you're in a green-coded time slot, you could take the time to address it. Yellow or red, probably not. If the interrupt is below the line, then you need to jump on it. Very few things, it turns out, are below the waterline.

Where you draw the line ties back to the goal-setting processes we talked about in chapter 3. As I go through my Sunday evening calendar review, I always have my goals in mind. What do I want to accomplish over these next ten days? My near-term goals list is neatly filed in my mind and nowhere else, but many of the performers I coach write theirs down and update them alongside their calendars. Victor Zhang, for example, is the chief investment officer and a senior vice president at American Century Investments, a large global asset management firm. He keeps a spreadsheet updated with his goals for the next one, three, and six months across all aspects of his life: work, health, family, spirituality, hobbies, and friends. When he's working on his calendar and future plans, Victor consults this spreadsheet. "Every week I take the time to plan what do I do now, what can I delegate, what do I do later or never," he says. Victor goes a step further with his goals and planning: "I carry two notebooks, one for professional, one for personal. I use them to keep track of things I need to be doing, short-term goals. I enjoy the feeling of crossing things out in a physical book."

This may seem counterintuitive, but the disciplined approach to time management that high performers like Ted, Alex, and Victor practice ends up reducing stress. I find that once I complete my Sunday evening calendar review, I can relax; in fact that's what I have scheduled in my calendar! I'm not overwhelmed by how much I have to get done, because I know that I am set up to make the most of my twenty-four hours per day for the next week and a half. When I wake up in the morning, I have fewer decisions to make, since I know what my day holds and how I will use my time. When stuff comes up, it's no big deal; I have a process for reacting and adjusting so that I don't let small stuff distract me from big stuff. I have time set aside to take care of myself and my family, and to enjoy the life I have so carefully constructed. This all adds up to a level of calmness that many people, as I observe, don't seem to have.

THE BARISTA TEST

A few years ago I was working with a well-known athlete, someone who competes in a sport that is frequently on TV. He had been struggling for the past few games, which is not unusual for even the very best athletes. One morning in the midst of the slump, my client stopped by a favorite local café to pick up a coffee before heading to practice, and the barista recognized him. Nothing unusual so far.

But then the barista proceeded to diagnose my client's recent performance issues. It turns out the barista was a former athlete himself and had played the same sport as my client in high school. This, apparently, made him an expert. He had seen my client recently on TV and knew exactly what the problem was. In between taking my client's payment and fetching his coffee, the barista demonstrated what he thought my client should be doing differently. Position your legs this way, start your move that way, here's your latte, and have a nice day!

My client got in his car and resumed his trip to practice. He thought about what the barista had said. A lot. By the time he got to practice, he rushed up to a coach and insisted they change this and that about his technique. Like, now! The barista was right! This was the key to ending his slump. Fortunately, cooler heads prevailed. The best way to review and adjust this performer's techniques was to rely on data and insights from well-qualified sources. The barista wasn't an expert; a former high school player is not qualified to tell a world-class performer how to change his game. And his ideas were based on a very small sample set of observations. I saw your game last night, and based on that I have an idea on how to fundamentally change your technique? Not a good plan.

The coaches showed my client other information—video, data, analysis, things they had tried already—which reminded him to trust their input, not the barista's. Pretty soon he was back on track, and his game has only improved since then.

(In all fairness to the barista, people probably tell him how to do his job all the time. Don't make the coffee too hot, more foam—oops, not that much, a little less sugar, and a little more syrup. Spend any time in your local Starbucks and you will hear *lots* of coaching! That coaching is warranted, since people know what they like in their drinks better than the barista. Still, it must get tiring.)

All of the performers I have worked with across a variety of fields have a process, full of routines they follow to pursue their crafts and careers. Their processes help them manage their approach to practicing, training, nutrition, learning, relationships, traveling, communicating . . . pretty much every aspect of their lives. You are no different: you are a performer and you have routines you follow in pursuing it. Most people, including many of the world-class performers I have worked with, start with a process forged from a variety of inputs. They might establish a practice routine in high school, a study routine in college, or a work routine at their first job. It may be a carefully constructed process, established from years of experience, or something that just sort of happened. You

were going along, living your life, when—what do you know?—
you have a process. It may not be intentional, but there it is: the
steps you take pre-, during, and post-performance. I don't need to
tell you or anyone else with whom I work to establish your process,
since you already have it. What we need to do now is determine
how you improve that process so you can improve your results.

Trust the process, I tell my clients, which is something you often hear top performers say. Follow the process and the outcomes
take care of themselves. But the process is not static; to achieve
optimum performance, it needs to constantly iterate. Follow the
process, track the outcomes, learn, adjust, repeat.

Doing this well requires good input, but now more than ever
there's a lot of noise out there. In scientific and engineering terms,
our signal-to-noise ratio is very low. The internet has given voice
to billions of people, and our phones and other devices deliver
that cacophony of opinion into our hands practically twenty-four
hours per day. So the first step to adjusting your process so you can
constantly improve is to figure out which sources of information
you can trust (signal), and which to ignore (noise). Trusted sources
should be *vetted*, with sufficient expertise and experience and putting your interests first. And their feedback should be *valid*, based
on solid evidence.

"YOU MIGHT WANT TO LISTEN TO HIM"

Pete Naschak moved all over the world during his career as a Navy
SEAL. One time, when he was deployed in Iraq, he spotted a fellow

SEAL talking to an experienced Iraqi ally. The young SEAL was giving a list of orders to the Iraqi, who was trying to explain why some of the instructions wouldn't work in that particular situation. They were both getting quite exasperated when Pete approached the conversation. "The SEAL was new, having just been deployed," Pete recalls now. "I asked him, how many missions have you been on here? How many in actual combat? The answer was none. Then I asked the Iraqi, and he replied that he had been on about two hundred missions. So I told the young SEAL, you might want to listen to him. He may know what he's talking about."

Although he probably wouldn't use this language, Pete was applying the principles of information filtering on the fly. He had quickly summed up the situation and determined that the Iraqi soldier was far more experienced, so in all likelihood a more vetted source of valid information, than the relatively inexperienced American. "Every mission is different," Pete says. "You have to be careful running a template. You have to think beyond training and understand the actual environment. Step back, listen, observe, pay attention, and learn what is really happening. I try to ask people what has happened before, which helps me build a framework to understand. I ask lots of questions, so I can figure out who is knowledgeable." This was a standard part of Pete's process at the outset of every mission: he actively sought out and vetted information sources to determine which he should rely upon. For example, the more experienced Iraqi soldier.

Top performers build a trust map of all the various nodes of information that are available to them. In fact, it's not just top performers, it's all of us. There are the news sources that you trust: National Public Radio, the *Wall Street Journal*, Fox News, the BBC, Al

Jazeera, CNN, social media influencers, a favorite blog, YouTube channel, or podcast, your local newspaper site. And those that you don't: the random clickbait that pops up in your feed with details about some salacious story you really don't need to hear (but sometimes click on anyway). This is collectively known as our media diet, the total set of information and entertainment we consume, and like any diet it is full of stuff that is good for us and some that isn't. Everyone has an opinion: media (social and traditional), websites, and your family, friends, teammates, and baristas. The trick is to filter the vetted from unvetted. Think about where you are getting good, solid feedback. And are you getting it regularly?

Start with the people to whom you listen. Who have you vetted to provide you trusted input? The criteria to consider:

- Loyal: is committed to your success through your ups and downs. They may have their own agenda. For example, your boss will be more successful when you succeed, but the good ones are equally (or more) invested in making you better. (Thought experiment: If a perfect opportunity comes up for you outside your current role or company, would your boss support you in taking it? If so, that's someone who's on your side.)
- Honest: will tell you the truth from their perspective, not just what you want to hear. They sometimes put the tough in tough love.
- Knowledge: can read you well. They see the nuance in your performance and personality and understand the bigger picture of your life.

- Challenging: pushes you, physically, spiritually, and intellectually.

When you look at that list of criteria, you may conclude that assembling a set of vetted sources isn't easy. I need to find a whole team of people who are not only loyal and honest but experts in my field? This happens naturally for athletes, who have access to expert coaching starting in their early teens. For the rest of us, it's more challenging. One option is to hire your sources, such as personal trainers or executive coaches. I also advise people to seek out mentors from their field, people who are experts in the field and may also know you and your track record. Former or current colleagues are a great place to start; that regular lunch you have with a colleague could turn into a more formal peer coaching relationship where you advise and help each other. Also, business groups and forums, who may have members with similar experiences and challenges.

As you form your team of coaches, mentors, and trusted friends and family, hold them accountable. Remind them of their role as your trusted coach, and ask them to provide you the input you need. For some people (coach, manager) this is their job. For others (friends, family, mentors) they may need to be reminded from time to time that you value and need their honest input. Don't be afraid to do this! While we all know people who never hesitate to give us their honest opinion, we likely know more who do hesitate. Once you have vetted your sources, solicit their honest input frequently. They don't help you if all they do is praise and agree with you.

We all have plenty of media sources as well. Which of those

can you trust? Use the same criteria as when vetting people: loyal, honest, expert, and challenging. It might help to ask your vetted sources (the people) what they read and trust. And to ask yourself, which sources scratch your itch to learn? Periodically review your media sources to eliminate those that are wasting your time by providing more noise than signal.

Just as most everyone already has a set of processes by which they run their lives, most people already have a network of sources who provide them input. Like their routines, these networks mostly evolved organically, without a lot of thought and intent. Take the time to vet (or revet) your nodes to assess how much you trust them. The information they provide is the fuel to your constant improvement.

Even vetted sources may provide invalid feedback. Your parents may know you better than anyone else. They probably put your happiness and well-being above everything else. And they will give it to you straight no matter the situation. But do you go to them for dating advice? Or thoughts on how to nail that presentation? They are great, highly vetted nodes of input, but the advice they might provide about your romantic ventures and presentation efforts might not be valid. When they tell you that the last one looked nice and why don't you get married and have kids already, their feedback isn't based on evidence or expertise. It's based on a desire for grandchildren.

This is particularly true for post-performance (and post-date) feedback. Emotions are running higher, opinions are flowing more freely, so your vetted sources are more likely to give you invalid feedback. Be aware of this! Make sure the feedback they are providing is based on evidence (they witnessed the performance, they have some direct knowledge of the outcome) and expertise (they know what they are talking about). This applies to self-assessment as well. Negative self-talk can peak immediately after a performance—lots of shouldas!—so that might not be the best time to objectively analyze what happened. Most of the performers I have worked with have a deliberate routine after a performance to assess how they did. They will set aside a block of time, usually long enough after the performance to let the emotions settle but not so long as to forget the details, and make sure to quiet the self-talk before they jump in.

Alex Myers is a professional esports competitor and former Red Bull athlete. His game of choice is *Street Fighter*, which is about—no surprise—street fighting. Alex fell in love with gaming when he was a kid and his mom got him a console, and he started competing as a teenager. Now, besides doing his day job as a talent agent, Alex travels the world playing *Street Fighter* and, as he puts it, "kicking some ass." (I assume he means digitally. Alex is too nice a guy to be a real street fighter.) I met Alex at a Performing Under Pressure camp and started working with him shortly thereafter. He was working through some tendonitis and wanted to revamp his approach to training and performance.

Before Alex and I started working together, Alex reported that after a match "I wouldn't want to look back on the details or study tape. I felt like it was like reliving a bad memory. I really had a hangup about it." Alex was a vetted source on his own performance but not a valid one. The feedback he gave himself was based more on emotion (anger over the loss) than evidence (analysis or how it happened). We worked on that, so now when Alex has completed a match he has a routine to analyze his performance. "I take a break and rest a bit before I try to process what happened. Then, when I get into it, I try to break down *how* I lost (or won) rather than dwelling on *why* I lost. The why can be emotional. The how lets me pick it apart without emotion, so I can learn from it."

Penelope Parmes is a retired insolvency lawyer, a world champion ballroom dancer, and an avid visualizer, which she practiced long before we started working together. She uses visualization as a component of her post-performance analysis. For example, she had one dance competition where she and her partner came in third. "I wasn't happy," she tells me, "because I felt like I was (or could be) better than the couples who placed ahead of me. I was discouraged. In the next round, I watched how they danced and tried to identify what they were doing that I wasn't. Then I visualized how I danced and was able to step back and watch myself as a third party, comparing my performance to theirs. That's how I knew what I had done and not done and why they danced better than me." This is a more elaborate process than Alex's, but the intent is the same. One of the best sources of feedback after a performance is yourself, but first you need to take the steps to ensure your feedback is valid, guided by objective evidence and not emotional self-talk.

WHEN TO CHANGE

Professional wakeboarding is more intense and athletic than the stuff you see on your local lakes and lagoons every weekend. The pros get towed at speeds of about 25 mph, and they accelerate to twice that velocity as they cut across the wake to start a trick. Then they launch and pull off double flips, multiple twists, and lots of other fancy stuff in the air before gravity brings them back to the water, hopefully atop their board and not, as pro boarder Mike Dowdy says, "face-planting on what feels like cement!" Mike's family moved around a few times when he was growing up. He started wakeboarding as a youngster in St. Louis and got serious about it during their days in Michigan. At age sixteen he decided to move on his own to Orlando, Florida, to pursue a pro career.

Mike and I started working together in 2016. Back then, Mike lacked consistency. Like all performers, he had a process, but, as he says, "there was no rhyme or reason to my preparation. I just trained hard and if things didn't go well at events, I would change things up. I had no idea why. I just figured I had to change something."

So when Mike and I started working together, we created a process and stuck with it. I helped Mike become much more intentional about how he spent his time, filling up his calendar with slots for both mental and physical preparation. We set and tracked weekly goals, based not on outcomes (how well he did in competition) but rather on process (how much he practiced, how well he stuck to his calendar), and identified his vetted and valid sources of input (coaches, family) while filtering out the rest (social media). It didn't matter whether Mike won or lost: he stuck to the process. "Athletes are doers," he says. "We always need to have something to do, so the overall structure of the day becomes very important. I set the time to go to bed and wake up, I scheduled breathing exercises. When I lack structure, that's when I get lost in the weeds. When I have a routine, that's when I'm most stable."

I often tell my clients that to get better, amateurs focus on outcome while professionals focus on process. By focus on process, I mean to carefully and systematically assess and adjust their process, and trust that the positive outcomes will follow. When we started working together, Mike's process was secondary to his outcomes. When he lost an event or crashed a trick, he'd randomly adjust his routines in the hope that things would improve.

In all fairness to Mike, he was just being human. By nature most of us evaluate the quality of a decision or performance by its outcome rather than the process behind the outcome. We rationally know that sometimes you can do everything right and the result still comes out wrong. A good or even great process can sometimes yield a bad outcome. But so what? We didn't do well, so something must be wrong with our approach. Such outcome bias, which is sometimes called "resulting," is common across many different types of decisions and processes.[2]

We are also prone to "availability bias": the tendency to rely on information that's most readily available.[3] Recency bias is a form of this, since the most recent result is often more readily available. For example, a 2021 study of NFL bettors from 2003 to 2017 found that not only do bettors overweight the importance of the most recent game when it comes to placing their bets, but their overreaction is even more pronounced the bigger the magnitude of the most recent win or loss.[4]

Then there is action bias. Do something, anything, even if doing nothing may be the best approach. Here's a great example of action bias at work: soccer goalies attempting to block penalty kicks. Penalty kicks are awarded when the defending team commits a foul, such as holding or otherwise impeding an opponent or touching the ball with a hand, within the penalty area (a box painted on the field in front of the goal). They are also a way to determine the victor in a tied match, as we saw earlier with Carli Lloyd's anecdotes. The ball is placed on a spot centered eleven meters in front of the goal, and the offensive player gets to take a shot, defended only by the goalie. Penalty kick success rates at professional levels are high: somewhere around 75 percent of penalty kicks score.

When attempting a penalty kick, the kicker is allowed a running approach to the ball but the goalie cannot move until the ball is kicked. This means, at the speed the ball is kicked at professional levels of the game, the goalie doesn't have time to read and react to the direction of the ball. By the time they do so, the ball is already past them. So they have a choice to make: they can guess which direction the ball will go and jump that way the instant foot meets ball, or they can stand still. Data modeling shows that the better strategy is the latter: hold position in the center of the goal and attempt to block the ball from there. For example, one study concludes, "an analysis of 286 penalty kicks in top leagues and championships worldwide shows that given the probability distribution of kick direction, the optimal strategy for goalkeepers is to stay in the goal's center."[5]

However, that is rarely what goalies do. They almost always guess and jump, either left or right. This has become the norm among keepers because they are biased toward action: they believe it's better to guess and jump rather than just stand still, even in the face of research to the contrary.

Add these all up—outcome bias, availability bias, and action bias—and there is a powerful human tendency to act when things don't go your way. Listen to any sports talk radio show and you'll hear what I mean. These shows are full of people offering quick reactions to what happened in the previous game. If this or that player stunk up the place, let's yank them! Then they often play a quote from the coach, who preaches calmness, continuity, consistency, and process. The nonvetted, invalid, emotional sources scream for change; the professional opts to trust the process. (The knee-jerk reactionaries are often called Monday morning quarterbacks, a phrase first coined by Harvard football star Barry Wood in 1931. Wood was, naturally, a quarterback.[6])

When people are struggling, not doing well at their jobs or other field of performance, there is a strong temptation to make a change. The right answer, though, is to *not* act, at least not immediately. Instead, create and consult an empirically based feedback loop. Collect information about the performance from your coaches and from yourself, but make sure it's valid: quiet your emotions so you can look at things more objectively, listen only to coaches whom you have vetted (no baristas!). Examine your process and outcome: Before the sales call, how did you prepare? During the meeting, how did you cover things? What was the result? Once you have done this analysis, then you can start to think about what aspects of your process you may want to change.

If you decide to make a change, do so one step at a time. Blowing up everything and starting over might feel good, but it's rarely the best tactic. Instead, isolate one or two components of your process, adjust them, and see what happens. If you are trying to make a chocolate cake and it doesn't come out well, you don't change the ingredients, baking temperature, *and* baking time. That's just hoping things will get better. The smarter approach is to tweak one or two things, collect more data, then iterate again.

While you consider change, remember that the correct thing to do might be to not change anything. Hot streaks and slumps both come to an end, as performance naturally regresses toward a mean.

Bad outcomes can come from good processes. Poor performers react to those bad outcomes; good ones don't. Nathan Chen made a few mistakes during warm-ups before the 2022 Olympics men's long program. The old Nathan might have made a change after those stumbles, altering his program or overconcentrating on those particular parts of the program during the competition. The new Nathan brushed them off and stayed consistent to his process. His attitude had completely transformed. The mistakes weren't something to fret about or react to. He knew they were rare and was happy to have them out of the way.

The hallmark of top performers is consistency. They love and hate change. Love because they constantly want to improve, and change can be a catalyst for improvement. Hate because their process is paramount, and any changes to it must be approached warily. Changing the process is serious, only done based on vetted and valid input, removed from the emotion of natural human outcome biases, and usually approached incrementally, changing one thing at a time rather than blowing the whole thing up.

I think of fishermen. When they are planning to try a particular region or river, they may conduct some research on where the fish are biting and what sort of bait or fly to use. When they get to the water, they will have a process. Survey the water, pick a spot, pick a bait or fly, and give it a shot. Try enough times to know that something isn't working, then adjust one thing, either the location, the bait, or something else. Change one thing, try it again, then change again. This might sound slow and frustrating; fishing isn't for everyone! But it's how top performers do it. They stick to their process, and make changes carefully. Patience is important. You won't develop a winning process overnight.

FAILURE AS PIVOT

Derrick Walker is a successful person who has failed a lot. He grew up in Detroit, the son of an engineer father and social worker mother, and excelled at both sports and music through high school. He played college baseball well enough to be drafted by the Arizona Diamondbacks, and played four years in their minor-league system before being released. He played with the Rockford Riverhawks in the Pioneer League (an independent league), then turned in his glove and spikes at the end of the following spring training. Failure #1.

From there Derrick decided to give the military a shot. He joined the Navy and eventually tried out for the SEALs. He did well at BUD/S, making it through Hell Week, which is the toughest part of the program. But then came the water exercises during the second phase of BUD/S training. Derrick struggled, and was forced to exit the program. He would not be a SEAL. Failure #2.

Derrick retrenched, got his MBA, and is now in the midst of a successful career as a finance leader at companies such as Nike and Nationwide. He and I started working together in 2022, and I soon discovered Derrick is an exemplar of a person who uses failure as an opportunity to learn and inform decisions and mindset. When I ask him about this he doesn't call them failures; they are pivots. That wasn't always the case. "When I got cut from the Diamondbacks organization, I was crushed and in tears. I kept asking myself, what am I going to do?"

That's when he started to hone his failing process. It starts with reflection. "I always think about the things I'm doing and what I could do differently. I was going to be a major-league player; I wouldn't consider any other options. So I reflected on the things I most enjoyed about baseball. I loved being on a team, I loved the camaraderie. I loved how baseball is a failure-based sport, and the tough mindset that requires. I thought I would get all of this from the military. Then, in the Navy it was mental toughness and understanding how to handle challenges, plus the idea of serving my country became more and more compelling. Then I was able to apply those skills in an academic and now a work environment. I'm much more confident in my ability to learn."

Throughout his journey from professional baseball to the Navy to graduate school and the corporate world, Derrick has developed a pivot process for failure. First, he reframes it from failure to pivot. He dissects the experiences that lead up to the failure, and reflects on what he liked about them and learned from them. Then he looks for what's next: where can he replicate the aspects of what he liked and apply the things he learned. It's a brilliantly simple, powerful strategy. When you fail, systematically list the positive aspects and learnings from the experience, then either change venues or try again. That way you never fail. You merely pivot.

THE WAKEBOARD ON MY WALL

The final event of the 2016 Pro Wakeboarding Tour was held in Indianapolis, Indiana, on August 7, 2016. Mike Dowdy sent me a text the day before the event: I feel good . . . I've been doing everything we put in place this week and have been consistent with my habits. I'm going to stick with the plan and give it my best effort. Then, the next afternoon, I received a photo of him popping a champagne bottle on the top of the podium. Thanks for all the help this year! I did it, World Champion!

Mike had superior talent. That was obvious when we first started working together. He was committed to success and a hard worker. Together we instilled process: a structure for managing his time, a clear set of trusted input nodes, and the discipline to stay consistent to his routine regardless of outcome. A few days after Mike earned his title, a package arrived at my home. It was the board Mike rode to his triumphant win, a fantastic thank-you gift. It now hangs on the wall above my desk. It's a wakeboard, but also a testament to the power of process.

LEARNED EXCELLENCE
ACTION PLAN—PROCESS

THE BEST PERFORMERS TRUST THAT IF THEY STAY CONSISTENT TO THEIR PROCESS, GOOD OUTCOMES WILL FOLLOW. TO DO THIS:

Get the most out of your twenty-four hours per day. Take time on a weekly basis to intentionally plan out every hour of your calendar for the next ten days, designating slots as green, yellow, or red depending on the importance and flexibility of the planned activity.

Improve your process by first identifying which information sources to use as input. Trusted sources should be both vetted and valid. Ignore the rest.

Vet information sources based on their loyalty, honesty, ability to challenge, and knowledge of your nuances and idiosyncrasies. Vet the validity of their feedback based on how evidence based it is.

Make changes to your process carefully. Base changes only on vetted and valid input, and approach them incrementally, changing only one or two things at a time and seeing how that works.

Have a defined process for how you handle failure, ensuring you both learn from it and pivot successfully to what's next (including trying again).

CHAPTER 6

Adversity Tolerance

Put them on a stage and ask them to
perform stand-up comedy, and they will
have a different response.

—Andy Walshe, human performance expert

In early 2016, my friend and colleague Andy Walshe called me with a suggestion. Andy was director of high performance (what a cool title) for Red Bull's 850 athletes and artists, entrusted with developing and running ways to help these world-class performers from a wide array of disciplines push the limits of human performance. Andy is a genial Aussie who, prior to his Red Bull gig, had held similar roles for the Australian Institute of Sport and the US Ski Team. He has dedicated his career to helping the best do better, primarily through pushing individuals outside of their comfort zones and helping them learn to tap their potential.

A few years earlier Andy had asked me to join (as a contractor, with permission of my Navy bosses) the extremely talented team he had developed at Red Bull, including experts from a wide range of disciplines (nutrition, strength and conditioning, physical therapy, coaching, and more). Besides working with the individual athletes on improving their performance, I also got to help the team with the many camps they ran. Most of these were skills camps to help athletes get better at their craft: skiing, big-wave surfing, moto-cross, etc. But once a year we aggregated performers from all sorts of sports and arts in our "crown jewel," the PUP camp. PUP stands for performance under pressure, and its objective was to help in-oculate these world-class athletes against the stress of performance.

The theory was to expose them to little bits of bad, stressful, or uncomfortable situations, observe how they respond, and teach them how to improve those reactions. These exercises would help them perform better when faced with the pressure of competition (and, in some of their sports, survival). This approach, called Stress Inoculation Therapy, is a practice first developed by Dr. Donald Meichenbaum, who broke the process down into three phases: ed-ucation (learn about the nature of stressful situations and human reactions), skills training (teach coping skills), and application (in-troduce stressors and practice response). Meichenbaum's research demonstrated that SIT is effective across a wide variety of stressors, including anxiety, anger, and pain.[1] It's sort of like a flu vaccine for stress: give them a little dose of the bad thing so the body can react and harden itself for the next, likely bigger dose. Biologists term this approach *hormesis*, which is when something that is harmful in high doses is beneficial in lower amounts. Or, as philosopher Frie-drich Nietzsche noted, what doesn't kill you makes you stronger.

In his approach to stress inoculation, Andy Walshe prefers to take performers out of their day-to-day life, explaining that "rather than addressing where they perform, we drop them in a different environment. With the feeling of pressure and uncertainty, they default to natural behavior, or beginner response. We don't run the risk of destroying your ego, because it's not in the area where you excel. I can't take a Navy SEAL and run a battlefield scenario. They won't feel stressed because they are so good in that environment. Put them on a stage and ask them to perform stand-up comedy, and they will have a different response." The exercises were designed to deliver high levels of perceived stress, while in reality the actual threat was much lower. This helps the performers learn their stress triggers and gives them the opportunity to practice managing their response.

For example, lack of oxygen is (with justification) a primal fear, but the mind can overcome this fear. Of course we have to breathe, but most of us can hold our breath for long after the fear starts to set in. In PUP camp, every performer goes through a breath-hold exercise, and in a few days most go from holding their breaths for 30–40 seconds to 3–4 minutes. Physically, nothing has changed. Mentally, they learn that their mind can overcome the fear.

As we got better at staging PUP camps, I started to see amazing progress with our participants. All of us, over the course of our lives, confront and deal with a wide variety of stressful challenges, from the mundane (traffic, work) to the profound (loss, hardship). Over time, we see how we naturally react to these situations and learn how to adjust. In each five-day PUP camp, we exposed our participants to a wider variety of stressful challenges than they would likely ever face in the real world, thereby accelerating the wisdom they would have naturally accumulated through life. And it worked: our athletes universally claimed higher confidence coming out of PUP, and their performance almost always improved.

The trick in creating these stress-inoculation scenarios was to create a situation where the perceived threat is far higher than the actual one. We wanted to trigger high-stress reactions, while never putting anyone in any actual danger. Sometimes this is easy: an athlete who is unfazed by a wave the size of a ten-story building or strapping on a wingsuit and jumping off a cliff may be terrified of talking about their feelings in front of their colleagues. Or by being dumped, like Indiana Jones, in a pit of writhing (but harmless) snakes. ("Why did it have to be snakes," said Indy and probably at least some of our participants.) Andy's request for me that morning back in 2016 was to come up with something new. "Mate, take a few days and think about something new we could do that would be epic for the athletes at this summer's PUP." Andy urged me to be creative. I mulled on this a while, and finally hit upon the idea of . . . and I don't know where this came from . . . a grizzly bear. It took some doing by Andy and his team, but within several weeks we had a plan.

Bart the Bear II is an eight-and-a-half-foot-tall, 1,300-pound grizzly bear and a TV and movie star, having appeared in movies such as *Into the Wild* and *We Bought a Zoo*, and TV shows ranging from *Scrubs* to *Game of Thrones*. When it came time to cast the bear for our PUP production, Bart was our first and only choice. Our people called his people, they lunched (probably over plates of chilled salmon salad), and pretty soon Bart was on his way to PUP camp. (Bart II passed away in 2021. He was unrelated to the first Oscar winner in the best ursine actor category, Bart the Bear.)

Our campers that year included nine athletes, four women

and five men, competing in fencing, surfing, skiing, long-distance running, BMX biking, and climbing. As soon as they arrived, the stress began. Day one included an ice bath dunk under the tutelage of Wim Hof (a Dutch athlete and guru who espouses the benefits of exposure to cold) and a short hike. It's been my experience that sometimes it's difficult to get high-performance athletes (or any elite performers) to concentrate on and fully understand the mental nuances of performance training, and that group was no different. They concluded their first day more relaxed than focused.

You know what demands focus? A charging grizzly bear. To paraphrase eighteenth-century British author Samuel Johnson, it concentrates the mind wonderfully.

Day two started with a trip to a trailhead, where we told the athletes they would soon embark on a seven-mile hike. But first, could they take some time to write about their experiences from the previous day? They took out their journals and started scribbling, when suddenly a "park ranger" came sprinting down the trail toward us shouting "Bear! Bear!" (We were on private property, not at a park, with full knowledge and consent from the owner. I don't know how real park rangers are trained to react to a grizzly bear sighting, but I hope it's not to run toward people while screaming hysterically.) Trotting along about a dozen yards behind the fake ranger: Bart the Bear II.

Like any good actor, Bart hit his mark, in this case a small piece of red fishing line draped across the trail about eight feet from our group. Whereupon he stood on his hind legs and let out a most frightening grizzly roar.

One never knows which of the three options—fight, flight,

freeze—one's body will choose when confronted with primal danger. Among our nine athletes that day, one fell to the ground and screamed, a couple pushed a colleague between themselves and Bart (fight, flight, freeze, or feckless friend?), and a few took off . . . in opposite directions. Mission accomplished: we had their full attention. These top performers may have thought they had built up immunity to their stress response, but Bart's charge dispelled that fantasy. They had just experienced the mother of all stress scenarios, and were now, once their heart rates returned to normal, ready to review their reactions, learn how to better control them, and beef up their mental toughness. The athletes met Bart's trainer and took selfies with the big fuzzball, then we got to work learning and practicing stress tolerance techniques.

WHAT IS MENTAL TOUGHNESS?

When you hear the term *mental toughness*, what comes to mind? How would you explain it to someone? Poise or staying cool under pressure, confidence, composure, focused: all accurate descriptors I have heard that add up to the ability to handle and mitigate the human fight, flight, or freeze stress response. The problem with these words is that they all describe an end state, but not how to get there. If I ask you to describe physical toughness, you can likely describe the end state (strength, resilience, and so on), as well as the way to get there (rigorous training, exercise, pushing yourself). You know what to do. What about mental toughness? What's the training and exercise for that? Besides being chased by a bear?

Everyone experiences stress. (Technically what we experience are stressors, which lead to the human stress response. Stressors + human stress response = stress.) Excellence stems from how well you react to it, how you maintain your ability to think clearly, make decisions, and act. This is the foundation of elite performance, but elite performers are not born with this ability. The best athletes, performers, businesspeople, leaders, and soldiers all start with the same innate stress response we all have, but as they grow they get help and practice in overcoming it.[2] They have the support of parents, coaches, mentors, and fellow performers, and have lots of chances to perform from a young age, learning how to overcome (or buckle under) pressure and get better at handling it. They pick up stress inoculation, mostly unintentionally, through trial and error.

Many of us don't have the benefit of this tutelage and practice, not to mention a summer camp that programs a charging grizzly activity between kickball, arts and crafts, and archery. But we can still all learn how to get better at handling the human stress response; we can practice mental toughness. This chapter includes a series of exercises to help you get better at handling the human stress response, so you can call on mental toughness when stressful scenarios arise.

I originally developed the framework for these for the Navy SEALs and made them part of BUD/S training for all SEAL candidates. Back then we just had four exercises (Goal Setting/Segmenting, Visualization, Arousal Control, and Self-Talk) and we called them "The Big 4." Since then I have added several more exercises, based on my work with thousands of business leaders, first responders, and elite athletes. Through understanding and practicing these exercises, you will learn to handle stress and even turn it to your advantage. They include:

- Visualize
- Plan for contingencies
- Be self-aware
- Breathe 4444
- Crank the dimmer switch
- Segment goals
- Counter fixed beliefs
- Black-box it
- Unpack the box
- Remember team

The consequences of not learning how to manage stress can be dire; it's often not just losing a game or doing poorly on a test. John Marx was a police officer for twenty-three years, nineteen of which were as a hostage negotiator on the SWAT team, and experienced a lot of stress and trauma in that time. "I was a patrol officer and detective, and in a lot of SWAT raids," he tells me. "I saw a lot of death, horrible murders, and other human tragedies. I wasn't equipped to handle it all. I was drilled in arrest control techniques, shooting, and driving, but that was all physical conditioning. I got screened by a psychologist when I joined the force, and that was the last time. There's no mental support system there, and we were afraid to ask for help because that was like admitting weakness.

"We learned the way to manage stress was to drink. There were times after the shift we'd go to a bar, drink, and talk about the day.

We intentionally drank to drown out the thoughts. I drank too much to cope with stress. That was my coping mechanism."

"After I retired from the force, one of my friends completed suicide. I had considered it; there were some dark times in my career that I had suppressed. When my friend took his life, I started talking about suicide with colleagues and learned that it isn't unusual. I figured, I have some life experience, I can do something about this." John founded the Law Enforcement Survival Institute to promote wellness, resilience, and effectiveness of law enforcement professionals, other first responders, and their families. He came across a magazine article about the tactics we were using with the SEALs and gave me a call. Since then we have worked together on seminars and other initiatives aimed at helping police officers manage the inherent stress in their work.

This is a stark example of what can happen when performers are not prepared to handle the stress of performance. But there are smaller, more mundane examples of the lingering effects of stress around us every day. The techniques I describe in this chapter are designed to help mitigate the real-time effects of human stress response in order to improve performance. They are not sufficient, though, to help people cope with more severe effects of stress, such as the kind John Marx describes his fellow police officers experiencing. That requires other mental health treatments.

FIGHT, FLIGHT, OR FREEZE

Go back to prehistoric times and imagine a saber-tooth tiger charging a pair of cavemen. Caveman Fred observes the charging beast and carefully analyzes his options. Caveman Barney scrams. Fred, a thinker, gets eaten by the beast and becomes the central figure in a *Flintstones* funeral. Barney, whose thinking takes a backseat to action, survives the attack and gets to pass his genes on to subsequent generations. He has developed what we today call the hypothalamic-pituitary-adrenal (HPA) axis, the fulcrum of the human stress response. While we may be fans of Fred, we are descendants of Barney.

The HPA axis is a body system that spots incoming danger and releases hormones to prime our response. It encompasses the hypothalamus (at the base of the brain), the pituitary gland (located beneath the hypothalamus), and the two adrenal glands (sitting atop the kidneys). The hypothalamus communicates through the rest of the body via the nervous system, controlling things like breathing, heart rate, and the dilation or constriction of blood vessels and airways in the lung. When the human body experiences stress, like a charging bear or tough interview question, the hypothalamus gets to work. It releases corticotropin-releasing hormone (CRH), notifying the nervous system of incoming danger and telling the pituitary gland to start pumping adrenocorticotropic hormone (ACTH) into the bloodstream. ACTH flows to the adrenal glands, and orders them to start secreting a stress cocktail of cortisol, adrenaline, and other hormones into the bloodstream. The sympathetic nervous system is now on full alert. This all happens quickly, faster than the brain is able to process what it is seeing and hearing. The body acts without thinking.

That's the physiology of the stress response. The reality is a bunch of physical and cognitive changes. Heart rate increases to improve delivery of oxygen to muscles and organs. Vessels constrict, so that blood stays with vital organs (caveman Fred can lose an arm to the saber-tooth tiger and not bleed out as fast). Blood pressure goes up. Pupils dilate to let in more light and improve vision. Small airways (bronchioles) in the lungs open up, bringing in more oxygen. Senses become sharper, and additional sugar and fats are released into the bloodstream, boosting energy. Muscles get tense, breathing gets rapid and shallow, and sweat and tears start flowing. Digestion slows down; why worry about it when you're faced with grave danger? (Robert Sapolsky, a prominent researcher of stressors and the stress response, notes that "if there is a tornado bearing down on the house, this isn't the day to repaint the garage. . . . You have better things to do than digest breakfast when you are trying to avoid being someone's lunch."[3])

Most critically, executive functions in the brain's frontal lobe diminish. Advanced problem solving, judgment, and decision making become impaired. It's harder to concentrate and remember things, thoughts race, and things get more confusing. Thinking takes time, a precious commodity when faced with imminent demise. Your body's HPA wants you to act, not think.

This was all an immense help back when fighting, fleeing, or freezing were the only options our ancestors had when facing danger and a second's hesitation could be the difference between life and death. Today, though, it's usually a hindrance. In today's stressful situations, we need to think and analyze on the fly, which is hard to do without a frontal lobe. We might need fine motor skills in our extremities, which is more challenging to come by with less blood flow. For example, the core competencies of Navy SEALs are their ability to shoot, move, and communicate. All of these are compromised by the human stress response.

Furthermore, there are a lot more stressors than there used to be. Our ancestors' lives were dull compared to what we experience today. Sure, maybe there was that occasional saber-tooth tiger skulking about, but there was no traffic on the commute from the cave to the hunting and gathering grounds and no bosses asking for a 360-degree review on how you threw the spear or created fire. The human stress response gets fired up a lot more now than it used to be. As Robert Sapolsky observes, when we get stressed over things like mortgages, relationships, or promotions, we "activate a physiological system that has evolved for responding to acute physical emergencies, but we turn it on for months on end."[4] Mastering the response isn't just important for performance; it can also be vital for health.

I think of the stress response like a series of dominos set up in a row. When a stressful situation triggers the hypothalamus into action, that's like tipping the first domino. All of the other dominos, from the release of cortisol and adrenaline and the accompanying physical and cognitive effects, are sure to fall shortly after the first one does, unless the chain reaction is somehow stopped. This is what stress inoculation does: each of these practices will help you stop the falling dominos.

VISUALIZE

Joe Maroon is a world-class performer who has worked with hundreds of world-class performers. Joe grew up in Bridgeport, Ohio, a big athlete in a small town. Not the biggest, though; his close friends included Phil Niekro and John Havlicek, both of whom went on to become hall of fame athletes, Phil in baseball and John in basketball. The three boys played baseball together, winning the state championship their senior year, and Joe made all-state in football and baseball.

(Joe's friendship with Phil and John both helped and hurt his athletic career. He played center field on the baseball team, an easy task with Phil pitching and John playing shortstop. "I had very little to do." When Joe and John showed up at Ohio State University on a football recruiting visit, though, legendary head coach Woody Hayes wrapped his arm around the towering John's shoulders and proceeded to personally escort him around the campus. Smaller Joe—5'6" to Havlicek's 6'6"—was left to fend for himself.)

Joe went to Indiana University on a football scholarship, proceeded to med school there, and embarked on a successful career as a neurosurgeon. He suffered a major midlife crisis in his early forties, when his father suddenly died and his marriage ended, prompting him to drop out of medicine and move home to Ohio, where he spent a year helping his mother manage the truck stop his father had left them. To help address Joe's ensuing depression, a friend suggested he try running. His first jog lasted a mile, after which he swore he would never do it again. But Joe slept well that night for the first time in months, and was hooked. Since then Joe has completed eight Ironmans (five in the Hawaii world championships) and he now regularly competes in and wins his age group in triathlon competitions. (Since Joe is now over eighty, sometimes he is the only competitor in his age group!) The physical activity helped snap Joe out of his funk. He went back to Pittsburgh to resume his career, and in 1982 started working with the Pittsburgh Steelers as one of their team doctors.

(Through his work with the Steelers, Joe has become an expert

on concussion assessment and treatment. We met in 2012, introduced by a mutual colleague, and he helped me develop proactive
postconcussive protocols for the SEALs.)

One of the athletes Joe got to work with on the Steelers was
star receiver Lynn Swann, who was in his final NFL season when
Joe joined the team. Lynn was part of four Super Bowl champion
teams, was Super Bowl MVP in the 1976 game, and was elected to
the Pro Football Hall of Fame in 2001. One of the keys to Lynn's
success, Joe tells me, was his ability to visualize. "Lynn was a master
of imagery," Joe says. "I would sit next to him on the way to a game
and in the locker room, and watch as he would visualize a play
over and over. He would watch the ball turning, and see the laces
spinning as he caught the ball, feel it in his hands, and feel how
he would move and twist to catch it. He constantly replayed in his
mind how he would move, until it was fully wired there."

Visualization is the common way to describe what Lynn was
doing, but he was doing more than just seeing the play. He was
experiencing it in his mind with all five senses: seeing, hearing,
smelling, tasting, and touching. Researchers call this kinesthetic
motor imagery (KMI); it's sort of like strapping on a virtual reality
headset and playing a game, except instead of just dialing in two
senses (sight and sound) you get five. It creates a motor program
in the central nervous system, fooling your brain into thinking the
event you are visualizing is actually happening. The brain literally
doesn't know the difference; you are wiring it for success, so by
the time you get to the actual event you feel like you've already
been there. Numerous studies have proven its efficacy, especially
in sports.[5] Practicing sensorization (or KMI) is a form of stress
inoculation: the first few times you experience something can be

stressful, but do it a few dozen times and it becomes old hat, and old hat doesn't induce nearly as much stress.

Alex Myers, the esports competitor, performs in virtual arenas, but when he plays he is often in front of actual audiences, sometimes thousands of people strong, with his foe sitting at a console right next to him. Like any performer, Alex has lots of pregame anxiety. "You sit right next to each other, so you feel the intensity of your opponent," he says. "What really helps me is visualizing with all five senses. I see the crowd, I hear it, feel it. Before I go to a competition, I find pictures of the arena, then I visualize being in there and hearing the noise of the crowd. Doing this has changed a lot for me. I have much more control of myself."

Alex told me about a competition he attended at the convention center in Toronto. "I used to let the noise of the crowd affect me. I wouldn't visualize it ahead of time, so when I got there it would throw me out of my zone. At that Toronto competition, I spent time visualizing the crowd, seeing the inside of the arena, feeling it. When I got there, I felt so much clarity. I was focused, tapped in, not feeling the external elements. I was truly in the game."

Researchers have developed a model called PETTLEP, first proposed in a 2001 paper, to help people practice KMI.[6]

- Physical—make the imagery as physical as possible. Don't just imagine the movements, do them. If possible, wear the same clothes you will wear when performing and use the same props (for example, a pickleball racquet).

- Environment—try to re-create the environment in which the performance will occur, either physically or in your mind.

- Task—be realistic when re-creating the task at hand; if your goal is to win your weekend tennis match, don't visualize winning Wimbledon.

- Timing—visualize the performance happening in real time (although slow motion may be helpful, too).

- Learning—incorporate learning and improvement into the practice. Don't visualize how you performed the last time, but how you will perform as you get better.

- Emotion—be real with your emotions during visualization; try to feel the highs and lows of actual performance.

- Perspective—people generally choose the first-person perspective when visualizing (how you will see it when you perform), although the third person may be useful as well.

If you have an important presentation coming up, for example, first rehearse it physically. Stand and deliver, just as you will in the room. Find an empty conference room (the closer in layout and design to the actual room in which you'll be meeting, the better), and go through the presentation just as you will with your audience later. Note not just how you do, but how you feel. What are you seeing, hearing, sensing? Then, later, perhaps on your way home or while relaxing that evening, close your eyes and go through it again. Hear yourself saying the words, hear your audience's questions and reactions, see and smell the room, feel your feet on the floor or how the chair meets your back. Let the emotions of success roll over you. Wire your brain for success, so when the actual presentation rolls around, you'll be ready and relaxed.

Visualization is an excellent stress inoculation tool prior to competition, but I also urge my clients to use it as a way to wire in the positive elements post-performance or post-practice. My rule is 2X: after a performance or practice, visualize your performance in your mind at least twice to imprint it in your brain. This is equivalent to practicing or performing three times, not just once.

This can apply not just post-practice or post-performance, but to everyday life. When we sleep our brain is consolidating our memories from the day. When they prepare for sleep many people are thinking about the things they have to do the next day, or perseverating on something that went wrong or is bothering them. Would you rather have your brain ruminating on those negative sentiments for the next eight hours, or on more positive ones? Every night, when I am getting ready for bed, I think back on something good from the day: what happened; how did it look, sound, and feel? It could be a good conversation with one of my kids, or a standout session with a client, or a talk that I gave that landed well with the audience. This is now a standard part of my nighttime routine: brush my teeth, put on pajamas, kiss and hug my wife, and visualize. Let all the aspects of that positive experience settle into my brain, and it's like getting an extra eight hours of practice.

Penelope Parmes, the lawyer and champion ballroom dancer we first met in chapter 5, practiced visualization long before we started working together. "I was working full-time and going to law school at night," she recalls. "When I'd get home I would go through the class and lecture in my mind and finalize my notes. That way, everything was running through my head while I was sleeping. It was a way to weaponize sleep."

Penelope does the same thing today, but now it's dance routines she's replaying, not litigation and contracts. "After a dance lesson, I come home and visualize everything. I'm in my body while I'm visualizing, trying to feel what I'm supposed to be doing. I isolate the moments when it goes right; my teacher calls them golden moments. In bed at night, I replay the golden moments so I go to sleep in a positive mindset. I find myself moving, my legs are jumping, hips are jumping. I feel the room, the temperature, the lighting, the floor, the air, the smells. I feel it all, smell it all, hear it all in my mind.

"After I do my visualization of the lesson, I always do a gratitude meditation. I review the day, take the time to be grateful for what I do, who I am. I visualize something that went well. It could be just one small thing, like I finally did a double turn correctly! I visualize that golden moment with positive thoughts." This practice has given Penelope tremendous peace of mind in how she approaches competitions. "It has made all the difference in the world to me. It gives me a mindset of confidence because I am prepared."

PLAN FOR CONTINGENCIES

Ian Walsh was practically born on a wave. The son of a sugarcane worker dad and schoolteacher mom, Ian grew up on Maui, Hawaii, playing all the sports kids play, but when he tried surfing for the first time he was hooked. In a bit of fortuitous timing, at about that time the Walsh family was forced to move, and the only place they could find was steps from a north shore beach. Young Ian came home from school every day, ditched his books, grabbed a board, and hit the waves. His parents' only rule was that he had to be home by the time it was dark enough for the streetlights to flicker on. When he got home, he picked up the books again. Bothered by the Spicoli-like stereotype of the dumb surfer, middle school Ian vowed to get straight A's and ended up graduating as valedictorian of his high school class. (Jeff Spicoli is a stoner, surfer-dude, scene-stealing character played by Sean Penn in the 1982 movie *Fast Times at Ridgemont High*. All he needs is some tasty waves and a cool buzz and he's fine.)

Now Ian makes his living surfing big waves at places with names like Jaws (Maui), Mavericks (Northern California), and Praia do Norte (Nazaré, Portugal). He and I met in 2016 and have been working together on his high-performance mindset and mental tactics ever since.

You might think that it's terrifying to stand up on a surfboard and ride down the face of a seventy-foot wave, and you'd be right. One way to control that fear isn't to think about what could go right, but to prepare for everything that could go wrong. Ian is a master of contingency planning. "Monumental big-wave days are infrequent, I can't control that," he says. "A swell in that range with good conditions, there's only a very small percentage of time when it comes together. When I have that opportunity I want to be in the water to make the most of it. What if I get smoked and lose my board on the rocks? I have to be ready for that. What if there are problems with the Jet Ski? [Big-wave surfers often grab a ride behind a Jet Ski, piloted by an expert, to catch a fast-moving wave.] I look for any possible holes in the process, and I put a system in place that allows me to stay in the water when speed bumps happen. It's a progression I go through to find potential problems and put contingencies in place. At the end of a day [of surfing], I look at what consumed a lot of brainpower on that day, then address that."

Ian was making a movie in January 2016, and one day the conditions were just about perfect. "It looked like it was going to be the biggest day I'd ever seen! I was out there with my three brothers, and one of them, D.K., fell. It was bad. We got him to safety in the channel of the surf and had to cut his wet suit off. He couldn't feel anything, and we were worried he had broken his neck."

Fortunately, Ian and his team had planned for this. "We had everything set up and already in place to get him safely to shore and to the hospital." Word came back from the ambulance that D.K. was OK, so Ian got back out on the waves, and it turned into one of the best days he's ever had. For Ian, contingency planning is a key component of managing his stress. "Nothing goes according to how you draw it up. I tend to operate at a higher level when I know the *t*'s are crossed and the *i*'s are dotted. Then I can just focus on performance."

To reduce stress, think through and have a plan for all the things that could go wrong, because things will go wrong. Have a plan A, a plan B, even a C or D. This is common sense when facing life-or-death situations like surfing a moving apartment building of water, but it's equally important and effective in handling any type of stressful situation.

For example, I'm not a big-wave surfer, but I do frequently

engage in a type of performance that is just as terrifying to many people: public speaking. To help calm my butterflies when I am planning for a talk I think about what I'll do if the screens don't work or my computer crashes. What if the microphone fails? Or I wake up that morning with a sore throat? Maybe these scenarios aren't as profound as having a loved one crash and get injured on a big wave, but in the moment they will be just as stressful. To mitigate that stress, I imagine the bad stuff that could happen and plan how I'll respond. What will I do if I have to give that talk without slides or a microphone? Or if I have to pause more frequently to sip my tea? What if I miss a connection when I'm traveling to the site? What is the plan B? And what if that doesn't work? What's plan C? These scenarios are stressful to imagine and plan for, but even more stressful to experience without a plan. Standing up onstage or in front of a client when your graphics won't present or your teleprompter stops working will trigger a human stress response just as big as Bart the Bear II did. Developing, practicing, and visualizing multiple contingency plans helps neutralize that stress response in the moment and provides a far greater sense of control and confidence.

Retired Navy SEAL Pete Naschak stresses the importance of being honest with yourself when contingency planning. "Lots of time people plan for perfection and everything going right," he says. "I would think about just the opposite, all the stuff that could go wrong. Sometimes your capabilities fail you or you have bad luck, so then what? The only way to prepare for that is to imagine and plan for it. What if I get shot in the leg? I would imagine what that would feel like. It will probably be worse than I can imagine, but I do my best to actually feel it. Things can go wrong—the enemy always has a say. This helps provide a framework and programming for a fast recovery from the immediate fight, flight, or freeze reaction. It becomes automatic, gets me to a place where I can think, get grounded, get moving again."

As a SEAL, Pete planned for some dire things. "What would happen if I got killed? What would that mean for my family? I had conversations about this with them, and had systems in place to make things easier if that happened. That helped me mentally prepare for going on missions."

Spend enough time in contingency planning and you will develop something called automaticity, which is the ability to do something automatically, without thinking. When you ride a bike, you don't think about how to do it, you just do it. That's automaticity. Automaticity isn't that important for slower-paced crises: when your computer crashes while working on a deadline or when you have a disagreement with a colleague, you have a few moments to think about what to do. But in other venues, it's the difference between life and death.

Anthony Oshinuga is an aerobatic pilot with whom I started working in 2018. He and his plane compete in an imaginary box in the sky, 3,000 feet per edge, keeping a minimum of 656 feet (200 meters) off the ground. As they swoop through various flips and twists pilots can experience enormous g-forces on their body, so, early in his competitive career, Anthony spent a lot of time visualizing how that would feel and planning for what would happen if he passed out due to G-LOC (g-force induced loss of consciousness). He also prepares for all the other things that could go wrong.

"It's a numbers game, all about energy management and vertical penetration," Anthony says. "Every maneuver loses a certain amount of altitude. I calculate the altitude gains and losses for each maneuver, then I visualize what would happen if I had an emergency failure." Anthony got to put his contingency planning to the test a few years back when he was training for an airshow in Coolidge, Arizona. "I was practicing a flat spin and suddenly there was smoke in the cockpit. I couldn't see much, I couldn't see the ground. I neutralized the controls, opened the canopy to let the smoke out, then I felt something warm. It was oil from the engine, running all over my leg."

Fortunately, Anthony had planned over and over for just this moment, so when the time came he reacted automatically. He got the plane under control and landed safely. "I couldn't pull out a checklist, I didn't have time to think. When you think you die."

BE SELF-AWARE

Be in the moment. Focus. Stay present. I'm sure you've heard these maxims and plenty like them. The problem is, life isn't that simple. While it would be nice to have just one stressful element weighing on our minds, most people have at least a few of them. When Anthony Oshinuga is preparing to perform his death-defying swoops and spirals in the sky, his mind might wander to thinking about how his portfolio is getting hammered in the market downturn, or what to get his mother for her birthday. When I'm getting ready for a talk, in the back of my mind I'm sometimes fretting about how my son did on his midterm that day, or a not-so-great conversation I had with my wife the day before. Excellence requires focus, the ability to put all of these concerns aside and completely concentrate on the task at hand. Any of us who have tried that, though, know that it can be challenging. Life gets in the way.

To get life out of the way, take on these distractions head-on. Do a "self-awareness" check-in. Review all of your circumstances—I call them mental performance vital signs—and note anything that might be affecting your ability to perform at your best. If you can, take care of them. More likely they aren't things that are easily resolvable, but you can at least resolve to think about them later, or remind yourself of the plan you already have in place. This will help isolate the distractions and prevent them from seeping into the performance.

Be honest and objective with yourself. There's no use in sugar-coating things! It's sort of like having a bunch of windows open on your computer, phone, or pad. That can be distracting, right? And must be a bit of a drain on the device, too. Reviewing your mental performance vital signs list is like going through your windows and tabs and closing the ones you don't need. It frees up your processor to work on the vital stuff.

I list eight different categories to examine during your self-awareness check:

- Life: finances, career, and the well-being of loved ones
- Sleep: Are you getting enough?
- Climate: What's the vibe in the workplace or home?
- Health: How is it? Any immediate issues? Pain, headaches, etc.?

- Mood: Are you on cloud 9, grumpy, somewhere in between?
- Substance: How is your consumption of alcohol, caffeine, or other substances?
- Concentration: Can you focus? Or is monkey mind your current state?
- Stress: How do these factors add up at this moment? What's the stress level?

Pilots use a checklist like this before flights, as do many of the SEALs with whom I have worked. It's a way of addressing all of the other stressors in life before going into the main event. Reviewing the vital signs doesn't mean you have to take care of all the other stressors in your life, but self-awareness in itself helps mitigate the human stress response. Practice volition: develop a routine to take inventory of your mental vital signs, address what's addressable, and put aside the other stuff for now.

BREATHE 4444

I give talks to law enforcement groups around the US and work with several on mental performance programs, which has given me the opportunity to get to know many dedicated, impressive individuals. At the top of that list has to be Deena Ryerson, the senior assistant attorney general at the Oregon Department of Justice. Deena has a fascinating background: she was raised in Utah, the daughter of Palestinian parents who had immigrated to the US from Jerusalem, and attended Catholic schools through her formative years. ("I have the cornerstone of guilt," she says with a smile.) She moved to Oregon to get her undergraduate degree, then opted for law school, intent on specializing in anything but criminal law and on becoming anything but a trial attorney. She went into private practice after law school and hated it, but somewhere along the way she participated in a "be a DA for a day" program and guess what? Loved it! She decided to become a trial attorney working in criminal law after all, and is now Oregon's one and only traffic safety resource prosecutor. That means she advises DAs and police officers around the state on prosecuting traffic-related crimes (like DUIs and vehicular manslaughter), and also works with legislators on traffic-related laws.

Deena tells me about a particularly challenging case she worked on that involved a car crash in which the passenger was killed. The driver was on trial for reckless driving, driving under the influence, and manslaughter. Deena was not just an adviser in this case; she was co-counsel in prosecuting it. The trial turned out to be quite stressful, with a particularly challenging and ornery opposing attorney and a lot of small-town politics. When it came time to deliver the closing argument, Deena was ready. She was also exhausted, having spent the last two weeks working on the trial practically around the clock. In the moment when she stood up to address the jury, all of that fatigue and stress caught up with her. "I drew a complete blank," she says. "I looked at my co-counsel, and said I don't remember anything, I don't want to do this, I'm so tired." Fortunately, this wasn't the first time such a thing had happened to Deena. It's part of her stress response. "I've learned over the years this can happen to me when I'm really nervous."

Deena's next step in that moment of high stress was something

I hear from my clients every day. She breathed. In for four seconds, out for four seconds, then again, again, and again. These deep breaths, which took only a minute or so, completely reset her body and her mind. It stopped the dominoes. Then, she asked herself a powerful question: "When this is over, what will you regret?" Her answer is that she would regret being wrapped up in the fear she was feeling at that moment. She would regret letting that fear get in her way of performing to her very best. With that clarity, she took a few more deep breaths and was ready to go.

What are you doing right now? Breathing. It is the first and last thing you do in life, which is why it is surprising that you probably aren't very good at it. Oh sure, you do it well enough to, you know, survive, but when you get into a stressful situation, all bets are off. How many of you hold your breath when things get tough? Yep, me, too. This is why one of the most effective things you can do to combat the stress response is also the simplest one: breathe, deeply and regularly.

Earlier in the chapter we covered what happens when a stressor event activates the sympathetic nervous system and the human stress response kicks in. These effects are reversed by the parasympathetic nervous system, which gets to work after the stress moment passes to help get things back to normal. The sympathetic system is like hitting the accelerator in a car, revving you up to meet the moment. The parasympathetic system is the brake. It returns the heart rate to normal, gets digestion working again, and vascularizes the system, opening up the vessels so blood can flow more normally. Breathing deeply is the one thing a person can do in the moment to activate the parasympathetic system. It's sort of like taking Valium or other pharmaceuticals that control the stress response biochemically, but it's free, immediately available, fast acting, and doesn't have a list of potential side effects that includes dizziness, drowsiness, and drooling.

Virtually any performer in any realm cites deep breathing as a primary tool to cope with a stressful situation. Research shows that when practicing deep breathing, the ideal respiration rate is around six breaths per minute, or one every ten seconds. (Normal resting respiration rate for adults is twelve to sixteen breaths per minute.) This rate optimizes heart rate variability (HRV), which is how much the timing between each heartbeat varies (and is tracked by most smart watches). Although it sounds like a bad thing ("Wait, you mean my heartbeats aren't perfectly timed?"), in fact most everyone has some level of HRV, usually just a small fraction of a second. Higher HRV is generally associated with positive health traits, such as fitness and adequate rest and recovery, and with stronger performance; it is an indicator of the parasympathetic nervous system in charge. Lower HRV is an indicator of a body under stress or perhaps illness; the sympathetic nervous system is running things. The optimal HRV is relative—everybody is different—but it's generally somewhere in the middle, not too sympathetic, not too parasympathetic, just right.[7]

Ever take a deep sigh in the midst of a stressful situation or busy day? If so, you're already practicing deep breathing. Sighs are the body's way of resetting emotions and restoring a measure of calm. The problem with deep breathing is that, apart from the occasional sigh, we forget to do it. We're under stress, remember? So, just like any other aspect of performance, you need to practice it until it becomes something you do naturally, almost without thinking. That thing that is the first thing you did in your life and will be the last thing you do, that you do thousands of times every day? Yep, you need to practice it.

When I was with the SEALs we employed a practice routine we call 4444 breathing: breathe in for four seconds, breathe out for four to six seconds (the exhale is just a bit longer), for four minutes, four times per day. Remember, the goal is about six breaths per minute. Now I preach this exercise to all of my clients. They put 4444 breathing in their calendars! You have breathed all your life but not like this, which is why you need to practice it until it becomes a natural reaction to stress. Your body will force rapid breathing and vasoconstriction; your mind will quickly and automatically counter with deep breaths and vascularization. Erik Spoelstra's Miami Heat team practices breathing before big games, such as playoff contests. "I give them something to think about," he says, "then we all sit together for a few minutes and they just breathe. Coaches, players, everyone's breath in unison. Before a big game, a pressure-packed game, there's a lot of anxiety. It helps to just breathe together." This reduces pregame stress, while providing a road map for what to do later, when the game gets tight.

An additional benefit to deep breathing is that it brings back a sense of control. Stress tends to trigger thoughts of things you *can't* do. Deep breathing is something you *can* do. I can't stand up there and make a closing argument right now, but I *can* breathe deeply. Focus moves from the stressor (the trial) to the action (breathing), which in itself reduces the stress. The dominos stop, and now you can reset and get to work.

Steve Pitts served on the Reno, Nevada, police force for thirty-one years, the last five as the chief of police. When he started his police career, there was no mental training whatsoever. "Just tough old-culture guys forming you through discipline and tough love," he recalls. In 2013, I led a training class for Steve and his officers, and he immediately started applying the adversity tolerance techniques he had learned. One scenario where he found them particularly useful was when he had to comfort the family of an injured or fallen officer. He would visualize the conversation beforehand and practice 4444 breathing, sometimes pulling his car over to the side of the road to fully prepare. These were hugely important moments. "When talking to the families, what I say is about them and their loved ones. It's not about the Reno PD or the chief. Everything I and we do is for them, and I need to do it very well." The breathing and visualization helped Steve calm himself, preparing him to be the best he could be for the families.

Joe Maroon, the Pittsburgh neurosurgeon, sometimes goes beyond deep breathing in his efforts to master stress. "Deep breathing is one of my rituals in surgery," he says. "When I'm in the operating room and things get stressful, I'll step away from the table, have a seat, and take several deep breaths. I reset my balance and get focused again." Joe tells me of one such time, a particularly delicate surgery where he was working with another surgeon to remove a tumor, that took even more than deep breathing. "I had to move the facial nerve because it went right across the tumor. It's like a thin piece of spaghetti, and if you damage it the patient is left with Bell's palsy for the rest of his life. [Bell's palsy is a condition where muscles on one side of the face weaken, causing that side to droop.] We were in the middle of the surgery, and I got very stressed. I stepped back, breathed deeply, but I still had a lot of anxiety. I told the team that I needed a break. I went to the hospital gym, ran on the treadmill for a few minutes, took a shower, practiced the breathing, and came back a new person."

Joe removed the tumor without cutting the nerve in about twenty minutes. "I knew if I continued with the anxiety I was experiencing I was going to have a problem."

CRANK THE DIMMER SWITCH

One day, Dave Wurtzel, the former firefighter and world champ we met back in chapter 4, found himself pinned to the wall by a hose. He was working with a team moving the hose up the stairs of a structure that was on fire. "We were trained to stand in a particular place when moving the hose line," he says. "That time, we were moving the hose up the stairs. I was improperly positioned and ended up pinned against the wall. Every time I moved the hose it rubbed against my air valve and turned off my air a bit more. Eventually it turned off completely, and my mask got sucked against my face. It was fine, not dangerous, but when someone asked me afterwards why I was standing there, I said I didn't know. I was making a bad decision. It ran counter to my training."

Another time, Dave climbed a ladder extended off a fire truck to reach a fire, and when he got up there he realized that he had left his backpack with his air bottle on the street next to the truck. "We trained in the summer, when it's about a billion degrees in Philadelphia. When we did ladder training, sometimes I took off my air pack before going up the stick [the ladder] because it was so hot. Later that year we had a big fire. I was talking with another guy about where to position the truck and ladder, then as we were getting ready to go I took off my air pack and put it on the ground! Because that's how I had trained in the summer. I was reacting, not thinking." Just like the time he had been pinned by the hose, everything turned out OK, except for the photo that appeared on the front page of the local newspaper the next day showing brave firefighter Dave Wurtzel hanging on the end of the ladder without his air pack. He caught some grief for that.

Dave attributes these lapses to his pre-performance routine. As in, he didn't have one. "I was just kind of swept along the currents, without a process to address what was happening. I'd get distracted by the smells and bells. There's an alarm that goes off when you turn on your air, and that became my trigger. I would get the stress response when I heard it but nothing to mitigate it. My mind would go all over the place, I didn't have an anchor. When things started happening I went into fight-or-flight mode, and ended up making decisions that were not very advantageous. I was everywhere but here."

Most performances are scheduled. You know when the curtain is going up. This isn't the case for first responders. "We can't schedule our moment," Dave says. "We have to perform when the moment occurs. We spend far more time as Clark Kent than we do as Superman. It's what you do in Clark Kent mode that gets you ready when you put on the cape. Wishing something is going to get better is not a plan, hoping is not a plan, you need to have a plan." My work with Dave entailed developing an entire routine for his "Clark Kent" time, and a ritual for how to prepare for going into action.

"Once I learned performance techniques," he says, "everything started to switch. My routine settled me down, so I could see everything moving around me, and could pause and make better decisions in the moment."

The screwups that Dave recalls might be termed as choking under pressure. He was a very skilled performer, but in the moment of performance he made important mistakes, despite all of his skills and training. Regardless of how skilled and talented you are, you will not perform at your best if you let your nerves get the best of you. You might choke. Beyond its existence as a popular sports fan complaint ("the bum choked!"), the term *choke* has a formal psychological definition: the performer wants to do better (motivation) and can do better (skill), but falls short, usually because of stress. All of the stress reduction techniques we include in this chapter can help reduce choking, but one of the most powerful is pre-performance routines.

Pre-performance routines may seem hokey, but they are in fact critical to reducing stress. They are like cranking up a dimmer switch, lighting up the body and telling it to be ready for the stressors that lie ahead. And like a dimmer, they can be fast or slow, depending on the person and the situation. We can *tell* ourselves stressors are coming, that we know what to do, we've practiced and visualized it ad nauseam. The physical ritual *shows* us they are coming.

The ritual should be something repeatable before every performance (every day at work, every important meeting, every challenging conversation). It can be as simple as a consistent meal (baseball hall of famer Wade Boggs ate chicken before every game), a certain song, or wearing a talisman of some sort, that lucky bracelet or T-shirt, or a leader's pump-'em-up pep talk. Snowboarder Toby Miller has a more complex ritual that integrates other stress inoculation techniques. He starts by stepping away from the venue before he competes, to give himself space for positive self-talk and visualization. "It's easy to start overthinking, so I detach and find a quiet place, even if it's a porta-potty. When they call my name, I retie my boots, zip up my gloves, and put on my headphones, which is a signal to my brain that it's go time. The second I hear the music, all the nerves and doubt go away and I almost feel like I have superpower. It's my cue to take a few deep breaths which bring me back to the present. Then I drop into my run and everything goes completely silent. I don't hear the music, crowd, or my board on the snow. Afterwards, I don't even fully remember doing the run. It's like I enter an alternate reality for those thirty-five seconds."

Marcus Luttrell used his "dimmer switch" ritual in the most stressful situation imaginable, the 2005 battle in Afghanistan. He was badly injured from gunshot wounds, his mouth was smashed up from crashing down rocky hillsides, and his teammates had been killed. "It still gives me nightmares sometimes," he says. "I was thinking through the details, throwing mags [ammunition magazines] in my shirt so the enemy didn't know I was there. The last one I put in was sticking to my neck. I had to sit down, go back to my training and conditioning. The problem was, the situation surpassed my training."

What got Marcus going again was his pre-performance ritual. "I have a phrase that tricks me into being that person," he says. "It's kind of my audio programming." Marcus's mantra:

Thousand Battles.
Anytime anything draws a breath or blinks an eye,

With my great powers come my great responsibilities,
Daily control, stay humble, work harder than anyone else,
never quit,
God above any and all things. Amen.

Sitting alone, injured, shot, and desperate in the Afghan wilderness, with dozens of nearby armed men intent on killing him, Marcus recited this mantra. Then he started mumbling the lyrics to the song he regularly sang to his team before heading out on a mission: "Hell's Bells," by AC/DC. Even in that most dire of moments, Marcus's pre-performance routine helped him reset and crank up his internal dimmer switch. He got up, crawled seven miles through dense terrain, and found refuge among heroic, friendly villagers.

SEGMENT GOALS

Let's say your boss drops by your desk on a Friday afternoon. "Hey there, happy Friday," she says with a smile. "You know that thing you're working on for week after next? I was wondering, could you also do this other thing that's even more challenging and time-consuming? And could you get that done by Tuesday? That's not a problem, is it?"

Well of course it is, you miserable taskmaster, you want to say.

You got it, you say.

Just writing this is causing me a bit of a stress response. My shoulders tighten, my fingers make more mistakes on the keyboard. Reading it may cause you a similar reaction. But when experiencing it for real, that's where the stress truly cranks up. You are instantly angry, anxious, and panicked. But you have learned how to be excellent, so you take several deep breaths to bring back your clarity and focus, and start to think about the task at hand. It's a big one! The stress starts up all over again. How the hell are you going to get this done?

Back in chapter 3 we talked about the value of setting goals. They help keep us on track toward excellence, and the very act of codifying them makes them more likely to come to fruition. There is a problem with goals, though: they can create stress. Once you've set an ambitious goal (or had one handed to you by your taskmaster boss), you are immediately confronted by the reality of trying to achieve it. This is why the best performers set big goals, but then they break those goals into manageable segments and tackle them one at a time. This helps you focus on something more attainable and controllable, and helps prevent being overwhelmed and stressed by the bigger ambition.

Segmenting is such a prevalent mindset among performers that it's practically a cliché. Think of all the athletes who talk about taking things "one game at a time." Or wellness programs that talk about losing one pound a week. Setting a goal of winning a championship or getting into swimsuit shape by summer can seem daunting and stressful, whereas merely trying to win the next game or drop the next pound is much less so. Once achieved, these incremental goals (sometimes called "proximal" goals, as opposed to the more daunting "distal" ones) build confidence, which strengthens persistence and motivation. They are a way of tracking positive progress toward the ultimate end goal, and help overcome the problem of not knowing where to start when confronted with a big challenge. After taking the first step, the second and third seem a lot easier. Goal segmentation also creates more of a process perspective (the steps) to performance rather than an outcome (the big goal) one. After you set ambitious goals for yourself, break them down into more manageable segments to reduce stress and increase likelihood of success.[8]

Goal segmentation works to reduce stress not only prior to performance, but also in the moment. In the middle of a stressful situation everything can suddenly feel much harder. I'm supposed to run up four flights of stairs in a burning building? I'm supposed to stand up there and talk for thirty minutes in front of a judge, jury, and audience? Yeah right, I'm out of here. But wait a minute. First, I'm going to stand up and take a few deep breaths. OK, I can do that. Now I'm going to approach the jury and say hello. OK, got it. Next, I'll recite the introduction to my argument. If that's all I get to, it will be fine. And so on.

Setting incremental, or subordinate, goals complements the practice of setting big-picture, ambitious goals. The ambitious goal is required to maintain motivation and resilience. Without it, quitting seems like a very viable option. Why go to all this trouble? But if all you have is the big goal, the inevitable failures along the way can cause irreparable damage to morale and confidence. For example, a 2008 study aptly titled "Eyes on the Prize or Nose to the Grindstone?" compared performances at verbal skills tasks between people solely focused on primary, big-picture goals (prize) and those looking at subordinate goals (grindstone). The result: "participants in the primary goal condition experienced the largest decreases in mood and expectancy."[9] Focusing on just the big goals leads to bigger letdowns. You need both big and little goals. Big to inspire, little to make the challenge manageable and keep up the confidence.

When Dave Wurtzel relates his story about the building fire scenario, he starts with his big goal of putting out the fire but quickly moves on to the achievable, subordinate goals. A fire is "a chaotic, unpredictable environment. I don't control what's going on. You have a physical load, mental load, time pressure, and heat. It gets to be over a hundred degrees in the suit, and my brain isn't working very well. I have to break things down. I can't think about putting out the fire. Right now I just have to move a few feet ahead and get through that door. That's all."

COUNTER FIXED, IRRATIONAL BELIEFS

My family has a dog. His name is Odin and he's a rambunctious and very friendly golden retriever. When I take him out on walks, most people are delighted to see him, breaking out in a big smile and frequently taking the time to pet him. A few people, though, shy away from him. I explain he is very friendly as I keep him close to me. They smile and nod but keep their distance. Sometimes they give me a short explanation, usually along the lines of "I had a bad experience with a dog when I was younger." This reaction is not rational: different dog, different dog owner, different time, place, and circumstances. Nevertheless, the person's reaction—their fear—is very real. They had a bad experience with a dog, it evoked a stress response, and now they have adopted a bias that they should fear dogs.

This is an example of something called the ABC model at work. Developed by Dr. Albert Ellis in 1955, ABC stands for Activating Event, Belief, and Consequence.[10] An activating event leads to a belief about the event, which has a consequence. The event doesn't lead to the emotional and mental consequence; rather, the belief formed by the event is what leads to the consequence. The person I meet while on my dog walk tells me that their previous bad experience with a dog (activating event) led to their fear of dogs (consequence). The past experience created a belief that dogs are scary, and it's the belief that causes their current fear. In fact, most dogs are not dangerous or to be feared, but that doesn't matter to the person who has already formed a belief to the contrary. As Shakespeare's Hamlet noted, "there's nothing either good or bad but thinking makes it so."[11] A person thinks dogs are bad; therefore, for them, it is so.

We all carry around belief systems that have been subconsciously formed by our experiences since birth. An event causes a change in our beliefs, which then becomes generalized, so a belief about that one event turns into a belief about a general set of events. *I got bit by a dog once* turns into *I believe all dogs might bite.* Learning from an event is fine and necessary: *I should be careful around dogs I don't know.* It is the generalization, or overgeneralization, that causes problems.

Our belief structure is inextricably linked with behavior and performance. Past behaviors and their outcomes affect our beliefs. Those changes become generalized, making it more likely that we repeat that behavior in the future. I did poorly on a math test or two becomes a belief that I'm bad at math or I'm bad at tests, leading to lower future performance. When we experience something as a result of our behavior, it triggers that belief system, and we accept the consequence without question. It happened before, which created this unshakable belief, and now that's just the way it is.

Top performers learn to question and control their belief system. We can't control past events and their outcomes, but we can control how we react to them. (The events and outcomes are not in our circle, but the reactions are.)

Let's say you accidentally drop an egg, which leaves a mess on the floor. This creates an ABC outcome: I dropped an egg, I believe I always drop eggs, and the consequence is that I must be a clumsy person. This is a sensible conclusion: if you believe you always drop eggs, then indeed you're probably a clumsy person. But do you stop to interrogate that belief? Do you in fact *always* drop eggs? Probably not. So your belief is what creates a consequence of clumsiness, not the event. All the event does is leave a mess on the floor for Odin to clean up.

Now let's say you drop that same egg, but this time you practice excellence. Crack goes the egg, oozing on the floor. Here comes the belief: the irrational conclusion that I always drop eggs. But now you consciously intervene with a rational thought: no you don't, I can't remember the last time I dropped an egg. I'm not clumsy. In fact, now that I've dropped this one egg, I'll probably never drop one again. I'm going to quit my job and become a professional egg juggler! Here I come, ESPN!

Fixed, irrational beliefs often show up as negative self-talk. When you make a mistake, particularly under stress, those negative thoughts may gain momentum, their irrationality threatening to turn that one mistake into many more. The way to stop this parade is to use evidence. "How many eggs have I actually dropped in the last six months? Just this one. Oh, right, so I guess I am *not* always clumsy."

Athletes, for example, can refer to their stats. An infielder making an error or a wide receiver dropping a pass both know how statistically rare those occurrences are, and so can counter any negative self-talk with empirical evidence. Negative self-talk can be self-fulfilling—berating yourself for a mistake leads to the next one. But so can positive self-talk, so when you screw something up, give yourself a break. Look at the evidence and take pleasure in telling yourself, I'm glad I got that out of the way.

The good news is we experience ABCs every day, and so have plenty of opportunities to counter the Bs and change the Cs. When an activating event happens, notice how your belief system kicks in. What self-talk does it generate, with what consequences? What happens when you intervene to question that belief and counter the self-talk? Do you notice an emotional change? Or a behavioral one? Practice this often enough and it becomes your new default mode.

When competitive dancer Penelope Parmes makes a mistake in the middle of a routine, in practice or in competition, she's hard on herself. Her fixed belief system kicks in. "I start to beat myself up and get frustrated. I tell myself I can't do something, or how it's so difficult, or how I've never been able to do that." She intervenes by telling herself, so what if you haven't done it before? You'll be able to do it, just not yet.

Penelope practices self-compassion as a means to counteract her ABC beliefs. "I read something once that said you should treat yourself as well as you treat your dog," she says. "You pet your dog, rub his belly, tell him that he's a good dog. When I get frustrated,

I stroke my arm and pat my leg and tell myself that I'm a good puppy. It settles me down and makes me smile. I remind myself I'm just dancing for joy."

Another approach is to talk to yourself as a good friend would. The friend doesn't have your ABC system, so probably doesn't react to a mistake with a fixed, blaming belief. Instead, they're nice. They give you positive feedback, maybe along with some constructive advice. Your ABC system wants to lock you into a lousy outcome, but your puppies and friends will help you avoid it.

BLACK-BOX IT

In spring of 2019, the US women's soccer team scrimmaged on a field at the University of California, Santa Barbara. Amid the passing, shooting, and shouting, one phrase could be heard over and over. "Black-box it!" players such as team captains Megan Rapinoe, Carli Lloyd, and Alex Morgan shouted at each other in response to miscues. I was a lucky spectator at the practice, and this was music to my ears.

I had the privilege of working with the team as they prepared for the World Cup tournament, to be held in France. I taught them adversity tolerance techniques at training camps in both San Jose and Santa Barbara, and one of the things we covered was how to compartmentalize negative events. In the middle of a performance, when things do go sideways or something unforeseen happens, put the event and its associated emotions and reactions aside so you can focus on the task at hand. The metaphor I use is to put things in a black box. Many of the people I have worked with, like those American soccer players, use it as a verb. They "black-box" it.

Black-boxing is one technique to negate the ABC fixed belief tendencies. Something negative happening in the midst of a performance will trigger the ABC model, spawning negative self-talk and emotions in a downward spiral. Alex Myers, the professional esports athlete, calls this getting "tilted," which is gamer-speak for getting aggravated or angry in the midst of a game. "This happens all the time in competition," Alex says. "I'm expecting someone to play a certain way, and it doesn't turn out that way. Something unexpected happens. When I'm tilted, I black-box the problem. Imagine a box where you throw any random emotion that flares up. Throw it in the black box. Things will happen outside your control; when that happens, you black-box it."

Unexpected things can throw a performer off their game and affect their ability to succeed. Black-boxing such mistakes allows you to keep your focus on the mission. If you are giving a talk or lecture and flub something up a few minutes in, thinking about that mistake will impair the rest of your performance. Compartmentalization—putting distractions away in a black box—lets you get back to focusing on the mission at hand. Once those negative emotions start flowing under the duress of performance it's hard to counter them, but I've found that the black-box metaphor is effective. It gives performers a mantra to use and an image to visualize. Others use different mantras or images: I once heard NFL star George Kittle refer to a red reset button that he draws on his arm. When he needs to forget a bad play, he literally presses his reset button. It doesn't matter what the mantra or image is, as long as you have something to use consistently. The physical act of saying the mantra (or pressing the button) and envisioning the distraction going away is what's important.

UNPACK THE BOX

After every game, Erik Spoelstra sits down with his Miami Heat team and together they analyze the notable things that happened. Erik calls this an "after-action review," the exact same term used in the military when I served. "What was reality, what was good, what can we learn, what can we do better?" he asks the team. "Getting into this routine helps get us out of the results-based mindset, and more into a process approach. There's always something to learn and get better. We encourage everyone in the building to be real and vulnerable, and have the courage to say if something was their fault. You start to get players more willing to admit what is bothering them. Get past that hurdle and you have a true safe space."

Lots of things happen in the course of a game—a missed layup, a bad call by the refs—that need to be put in the black box. Erik's after-action review is his way of unpacking the box and clearing it out so the team is ready for the game. The players and coaches review the events of the game from a distance, separated from the emotion of the moment by time. This gives them a more objective perspective, so they can assess their performance not to criticize but to learn. The reviews are an important part of the team's culture, and they can surface issues beyond what happened on the court. "Everyone knows what it takes to win," Erik says. "But once you start competing and get into the season things come up that will clutter that. Personal agendas, noise from the media . . . if you don't address this stuff it gets in the way. You need to be intentional about them." Erik's after-action reviews are his technique to keep the team from getting fragmented.

When you put things in the black box, at some point you need to unpack it. Review the salient events and emotions of the performance, good and bad, and objectively analyze what happened and why. Reduce emotions and remove recriminations to focus on learning and growing from the experience. When unpacking the box, make sure you are in a safe emotional space, away from people who may skew the process with judgment. Start by validating the emotions that you experienced in the moment; getting frustrated or angry at a mistake is normal and OK. If something went wrong and you had an emotional reaction, you may want to break it down by the ABC model. What belief triggered the emotion or self-talk you experienced? Was that a rational belief? Often, performance mistakes trigger emotions based on reputation: I made a mistake and now everyone will think worse of me. If that's happening, revisit the moment and center yourself on your identity and values.

Once the emotions are cleared, you have the freedom of objectively assessing your performance and improving it. Aerobatic pilot Anthony Oshinuga has a good example of this. "When I was starting out I was with a flight instructor, and we were practicing a maneuver called a goldfish. It's a really hard pull—I hang inverted from the straps for some time—and I got knocked out from the g's. When I came to, I asked the instructor if we could run through it again, and it knocked me out again!"

After every flight, Anthony has a post-performance routine that entails sitting in the plane and replaying what happened. After those knockout goldfish experiences, he knew he had to beef up his resistance to g-forces. "I spent a whole month studying what happens when you go through that kind of g-force, what happened to me, why I was knocked out. I learned that I had to work out more and get stronger, so that when I flex (as I'm going into a pull) the blood stays in my brain and I don't pass out." His routine of unpacking the box helped Anthony develop a plan to improve and reduce the stress of future flights.

THINK ABOUT TEAM

One final way to address stress is to remember why you are doing what you do. There are the factors we covered in chapter 3, where we learned about personal credo and engine. But there is frequently another component of purpose: team. In many performances, you aren't alone. You have a team around you and behind you. Reminding yourself of this can have a powerful calming influence before and during a performance.

I have observed this effect at work many times in my work with the SEALs. They are a community where the bonds of team are especially strong. SEALs care more about their teammates than themselves; their sentiments are on par with the protectiveness parents have for their children. When they are commencing a mission or exercise, they look at their teammates, knowing that the pressure of success does not fall entirely on their shoulders. They know no one will quit, they will have help every step of the way. Consciously reminding themselves of the presence and support of their teammates is both a motivating and calming factor.

Tim Murphy is a psychologist, author, and former US congressman, having served in the House of Representatives from 2003 through 2017. Tim and I met in 2011, when I was the lead psychologist for the West Coast SEAL Teams and he was a reserve naval officer (while serving in Congress). He was on board an aircraft carrier, the USS *Carl Vinson*, while it was stationed at Coronado, and called me up one day to see if he could come by to learn more about the SEALs' mental toughness programs.

Tim has always been an advocate for mental health, and he is especially proud of the family mental health bill he authored following the mass shooting at Sandy Hook Elementary School in Newtown, Connecticut, in 2012, several provisions of which ultimately made it through Congress and into law. He recalls the hearings for that bill and the political pressures he faced as he pushed for it. "The mark-up process for a bill is brutal," he says. "Some of my House colleagues were going to let the dogs loose on me." To help manage this stress, Tim kept his team front and center in his mind; in this case, the team was the people for whom he had written the legislation. "My bill was fueled by mass shootings, and I had talked to lots of victims and their families. When the hearing started, I had photos of all the kids who died at Sandy Hook on the table in front of me. This wasn't about me, it was for them. I wasn't pretending to be calm. I was calm. I was in a battle and it was game on."

Patty Brandmaier also mitigated stress at key moments by focusing on team. Patty spent thirty-two years at the Central Intelligence Agency, starting as an analyst and working her way through the organization to spend her final seven years as a member of the senior executive team, reporting to the director of the agency. She served both domestically and overseas, led several mission-critical initiatives, managed the CIA's relationships with Congress and the US Department of Defense, was awarded three Director's Awards, the exclusive honor bestowed by the director, and earned the Distinguished Career Intelligence Medal when she retired in 2014.

Patty was hired by the CIA after graduating from Penn State and loved it right away. "I could do anything there. I started on the analytical track, which I eventually realized I didn't like. My biggest challenge was to develop a disciplined approach to doing things I wasn't excited about. I gravitated towards things I liked the most. I moved around a lot and they kept promoting me."

Patty's professional journey included several positions of increasing responsibility and seniority in the CIA's Counterterrorism Center, so when the first plane hit the World Trade Center in New York on September 11, 2001, she knew exactly what to do. She didn't have the luxury of a stress response; there was a new team that needed to be built. "We needed to get organized, we needed to get ready for whatever might be coming next, to protect the country. While everyone was exiting the building, I headed to our Counterterrorism Center."

Patty was well versed in many of the stress management techniques I detail in this chapter, including how to channel her emotions during challenges. "I'm an emotional person," she says. "I've even cried in front of the director. Emotions are contagious. I've learned that the hard way. My emotions used to impact other people. One of my top leadership tenets is to understand yourself, and I had to learn what triggered me so I could manage those triggers." Suffering the 9/11 terrorist attacks was certainly one of those triggers. Patty and her team raced to set up a crisis management center, to help the country determine the threats it was facing, what was real and what wasn't. "We didn't know what was coming next. We were working twenty-four/seven, and people were scared. I knew that how I showed up in front of them was important."

Patty is correct: stress can be contagious. Mastering the techniques in this chapter will help you improve not only your own performance, but also the performance of those around you. As Patty notes of the 9/11 attacks, "I couldn't let my stress and anxiety become theirs. That's the way we could manage our stress together."

EMBRACE GOOD STRESS

To Dr. Joe Maroon, the neurosurgeon, stress and mindset are inextricably linked. "Stress is a good thing," he says. "We need it. To be a better athlete you need to work your muscles physically. Stress does the same thing to your mindset. It conjures up your focus and intensity when you are working on something. There is good stress and there is distress. The best performers learn how to deal with distress so they can get back to the good-stress mode."

Cliff diver David Colturi says something similar. When he stands atop his perch looking down at the water a hundred feet below him, he gets scared. "For elite performers the fear and stress is never absent. It's going to be there, so how can I use it? I try to leverage it as a motivator. If I have anxiety about something, like giving an interview or a talk, that motivates me to prepare more and perform better. Fear helps me get better day in and day out."

We have spent this entire chapter learning how to prepare for

and mitigate the human stress response. Mitigate, but not eliminate, because while stress has a lot of bad effects it has good ones,
too. Once you practice the techniques we cover in this chapter to
the point they become automatic, you will successfully eliminate
(or significantly reduce) the amount of distress in your life. But
there will still be stress, which is good. You now know how to handle it and turn it into a positive force for your performance.

Psychologists Alia Crum, Peter Salovey, and Shawn Achor call
this the "stress paradox." In a 2013 paper, they cite numerous studies documenting the positive aspects of stress, both in the moment
(heightened awareness, more focus) and longer term (increased ini-
tiative taking, new perspectives, sense of mastery, increased sense of
meaningfulness). These are the markers of "stress-related growth,
in which stressful experiences fundamentally change individuals
for the better." They go on to show that one's mindset about stress
is in itself a variable affecting the human stress response. Most of
us believe that stress is harmful; this "stress-is-debilitating" mindset actually exacerbates the negative effects of stress. It's our own
special stress-and-mindset vicious circle. On the other hand, flipping that belief around can create a "stress-is-enhancing mindset,"
which is in itself a stress-controlling technique.[12]

I'm not saying that stress is good. Sometimes it is triggered
by challenging life events that we are better off not having to experience. But regardless of whether the stress stems from major
issues, mundane ones, or something in between, it is a signal to
our body and mind that something important is at hand. This in
itself can be beneficial. Dr. Kelly McGonigal, in her book *The Upside of Stress*, notes that "stress is what arises when something you
care about is at stake."[13] If we get better at managing our stress

response, we set ourselves up for less running away and more step-ping forward.

Pete Naschak, the retired SEAL, has spent a lot of time coach-ing other high performers on mental performance, including sev-eral Olympic athletes. "It bothers me when they say that it's just another competition," Pete says. "It's not just another competition, it's the Olympics! It's like someone running around in the rain saying, 'It's not raining.' It's raining!" The techniques we have cov-ered in this chapter provide you with the confidence that when adversity comes your way, you are prepared to handle it. You can mitigate and counter the bad effects of stress, so you are more able to embrace its good aspects.

"Don't get rid of the nerves," Pete counsels. "Use them. Nerves are your body telling you, this matters. It's important to have a bit of fear. It heightens senses, keeps you aware, and tells you it's time to make something happen. When I'm on the battlefield, I don't want to be a Gandhi. Is that really the best way to be when you're in a fight?"

LEARNED EXCELLENCE ACTION PLAN—ADVERSITY TOLERANCE

MENTAL TOUGHNESS IS THE ABILITY TO MANAGE THE HUMAN STRESS RESPONSE IN CHALLENGING SITUATIONS. TO DEVELOP MENTAL TOUGHNESS, PRACTICE AND USE THESE TECHNIQUES:

Visualize upcoming performances with all five senses, so when it comes time to actually perform it feels like you've already been there. Use visualization post-performance, too, to review and learn from the experience.

Have a contingency plan for all the things that could go wrong. Practice it enough to develop automaticity, so you can act correctly in the moment without thinking.

Be self-aware. Prior to performance, take stock of your mental performance vital signs to mitigate distractions. Address or acknowledge factors across various aspects of life that may be causing stress.

Breathe 4444. Practice breathing, four seconds in, four to six seconds out, for four minutes, four times per day.

Establish pre-performance routines, a physical signal to your body and mind that a performance event is coming.

Break big, daunting goals down into smaller, more achievable ones.

Counter fixed, irrational beliefs, and their attending negative self-talk, with rational, evidence-supported, positive self-talk.

When something unexpected happens during a performance, black-box it. Mentally stow it away for now so it doesn't cause further distraction.

After performances, unpack the box. Review the salient events and emotions of the performance, good and bad, and objectively analyze what happened and why.

To inspire and calm yourself, think about your teammates before and during performances.

CHAPTER 7

Balance and Recovery

I talked about not having any jerks on the
team, but if I'm being a jerk then how can
we say we don't have any jerks?

—Steve Idoux, producer and president, Lockton Dallas

S teve Idoux always believed he would outwork everyone. That
was his path to success. "My attitude was, I will put in more
hours," he recalls. "I will answer your call at midnight, at five
a.m., on the weekend. I was always pounding Diet Cokes. I'm
tougher than you, I have more energy." One day Steve was in his
office at his desk. "I was a little exhausted from a client dinner the
night before. Something had happened with one of our clients
and one of my team members came in to talk about it. Suddenly,
I found myself yelling at him. I became this snarling person! I
remember the look on his face. I thought, I don't want to be that

person. That's not me. That's not what this company needs. I was passionate, but it came across as browbeating people. The irony was, as I started to get more successful I got angry more often. I wanted to be like Steve Jobs and never lower our standards. If I saw them being lowered, I would react viciously. I talked about not having any jerks on the team, but if I'm being a jerk then how can we say we don't have any jerks?"

I started working with Steve in 2019. One of our immediate priorities was balance. Steve was way overinvested in his career, and not paying enough attention to other aspects of his life. He's not alone in this trait; in fact, it may sound familiar to you. So many of us define ourselves by what we do, when in fact we are way more than that.

How much more? I count six "pillars" that make up a life:

- Work—your job and career
- Relationships—romantic, family, friends, and colleagues
- Health—exercise, nutrition, and other aspects of physical well-being
- Spirituality—belief and practice that there is something purposeful beyond our physical and mental selves. This can encompass religion, but nonreligious people have spirituality, too.
- Hobbies—things we do for fun, education, or community
- Legacy—what will we leave behind?

A whole and happy life doesn't derive from just one or two of these pillars; it draws from all six of them. I think of them as pillars holding up a house. A house built on just one or two pillars is always going to be unstable. If one pillar gets compromised in some way, the entire structure can collapse. But if the house has a solid foundation of four, five, or even all six pillars, it's going to be rock-solid even if a couple of those pillars are damaged. When people are out of balance, putting all their energy into just one pillar, failure has greater consequences and stress increases. If all you have is your job or career, you'd better knock it out of the park because you have nothing else going on. When adversity happens, balance helps you stay grounded. You have other things to fall back on. The best, healthiest performers I've come across feed and water their six pillars constantly (and none of them mind an occasional mixed metaphor!). There is no optimal, one-size-fits-all formula for this; it will differ for each person. The focus should be more on the process of balance (periodically considering how you are tending to each pillar) than the outcome (X hours on this pillar, Y hours on that one).

Sometimes when I was working with the SEALs, I'd occasionally hear a bias against balance. If you aren't solely and singularly focused on being a great SEAL, the thinking went, you won't perform as well. This is untrue. Balance improves performance. The best example I know of this is baseball pitcher Rich Hill, who is one of the most intense, disciplined, focused athletes I've ever worked with. I've seen him rally teammates with his intensity numerous times. But outside the lines, Rich exemplifies what it means to be a father, husband, and member of the community. "We have dinner together every night," Rich says of his family life. "When I get home, I leave everything at the field. When you are at home, you are a dad and husband. When you're at the field you're a teammate, a competitor, and a friend."

Ample research supports the importance of balance, which leads to increased happiness, better performance and productivity, lower attrition, higher job satisfaction, higher productivity, better health and longevity, and more creativity. For example, a 2013 study of 1,416 people across seven countries found that those with more balance in their lives are more satisfied and have less anxiety and depression.[1] And a 2009 review concluded that companies with superior balance practices have better retention and recruiting.

Balance is also important for successful transitions. I have seen many SEALs struggle after they leave the Navy while many others do just fine. The difference is usually in the health of their pillars. The ones who have fulfilling community, family, and spiritual lives always do better.

Back in chapter 3 we talked about setting goals across each of the six pillars. When my clients first go through this exercise, they almost always focus on just one or two pillars, usually work and relationships (primarily family). This is fine and expected, but not good enough. What are the things you want to work on and achieve in all six areas? For example, hobbies can include things you do for fun, but it can be helpful to pick something at which you want to get better—a new language, cooking, travel to a new country or region—and focus on that for a period of time.

The objective doesn't have to be to achieve balance in the short or even medium term. There are stretches of times when we have to go all in on just one or two pillars (usually work or family). In those times, be aware of the deficit you are creating in the other pillars and make the mental commitment to rebalancing at some point in the not-too-distant future. Plan a vacation, for example, not just for better and more family or partner time, but also to invest in hobbies, spirituality, or the other pillars that are weakening. This is critical for excellence.

Setting all these goals can be intimidating. It's OK to make the process a little less complex by doubling or tripling up in some areas. I might set a goal to play pickleball with my wife weekly (assuming she'll agree to it!), which counts as a health, hobby, and relationship goal. (Praying to the pickleball gods before the match does not, however, fulfill a spiritual goal.) As Ben Potvin, the former Cirque du Soleil performer and creative director, notes, "Being balanced is not a destination. You need to focus energy on your pillars all along the way and keep growing in each of them."

LET THE BALLS DROP

Even with doubling up the occasional goal, setting goals in six different pillars can feel overwhelming. It's hard enough to keep up with just your job and family, right? Deena Ryerson, the senior assistant attorney general in Oregon, recalls that when she was growing up "our generation said women can have it all. A career, a family, a life; all of it. But I've learned you can't have it all and do it all *well*. I tried that for years and I paid for it. I put everything in my career more so than my family, which I regret to this day." Deena was constantly shifting between her roles as an attorney and mother and feeling like she wasn't doing either to the best of her abilities. She would get agitated at things that normally wouldn't get to her. "You're not mad at the dishes, you are stressed by other issues."

As I started working with Deena, she came to realize that she *can* have it all, but not all at once. Raising two sons, she started to shift priorities and goals based on circumstances. "There are balls that have to drop," she says. "Once you realize that, you have to forgive yourself. I can't be everything I want to be for my job without sacrificing what I am for my family, and vice versa. Now, when the fire isn't at full flame at work, I take more time with family. I start with the nonnegotiables. If I have a trial coming up, that's a nonnegotiable. But I wouldn't have missed my son's homecoming game for anything; that's also a nonnegotiable. I line up the nonnegotiables, then see what's left."

When it comes to your pillars, timing is everything. Ages and stages change. Deena, in the middle of her career and raising a family, has to focus most of her time and energy on those two pillars, while new retirees or empty-nesters have the luxury of developing hobbies and community. It's OK to not be 100 percent balanced—time and attention equally distributed across the pillars—in any given moment. Which is good, because as Deena and many others know, sometimes it isn't possible. But be aware of the imbalance, make it intentional, and have a plan to address it when circumstances change.

Use the currency of time. We talked in chapter 5 about developing a time management process that ensures you invest your time in your most important priorities. To maintain balance, go a step further and label how you are using time. Build in time for work, of course, but also time for health, family, friends, spiritual reflection, and so on. If you color-code these, you can look at a week in your calendar and see the balance or imbalance. If there is imbalance, you can choose to adjust how you are investing your time, either now or in the future. Don't let yourself off the hook too easily. Striking a balance in the coming days and weeks may not be possible: balls are going to drop. But how about months? Surely there is space to invest in all aspects of your life within that span. This isn't a luxury; high performance now and in the future requires it.

When investing time and attention to various pillars, make an effort to avoid distractions. Being present and staying in the moment are clichés, but also vital to maintaining balance. It's obvious that a performer needs to be focused when in the midst of performing—you wouldn't want your doctor to be thinking about an upcoming date when in the middle of your surgery. But the converse is also true. Just as we want to eliminate distractions and be fully present when performing, maintaining balance requires the same discipline in nonperformance scenarios. How often do your thoughts stray to that important upcoming meeting or event when you are in the middle of playing with your kids or having dinner with your partner? A lot, right? This is an opportunity for improvement for most people. Put aside those thoughts of what's next and let yourself be where you are.

THE PATH TO RECOVERY

When Navy SEAL Marcus Luttrell returned to Texas after his ordeal in Afghanistan, I spent a week with him and his family, helping him to readjust to home life. A few days after we arrived, some of his friends appeared at the door. They wanted to help Marcus, and figured a good way to do that was to take him out for the day. Their activity of choice? Shooting!

Think about a race car. It's out on the track zipping around as fast as possible, but to keep going it occasionally needs to pull into the pit and spend some time recovering: changing tires, filling the tanks, checking the brakes or steering. At the end of the race it's back to the garage for more recovery, with extensive maintenance and retooling. Then it's on to the next race. The same was true for Marcus. He wasn't ready to pick up and fire a gun, even for sport. He needed more recovery. I talked with Marcus's well-meaning friends and we figured out something else they could do that would be fun while giving Marcus the much-needed time and space to continue his recovery. How about fishing?

A critical component of being an excellent performer is to provide yourself the time and space to recover from performing. Performing gets your stress response revved up; recovery provides a chance to cool down. Build recovery into your day, schedule it in your calendar if need be. Ex-SEAL Pete Naschak notes that he was often better at recovery when he was deployed, because he was more deliberate about making time for it. "I was more focused on that time off when I was in Iraq," he says. "Everything was focused, centered, and important, and there weren't any distractions."

Recovery is more challenging in Pete's civilian life, where there is more stuff going on around the house, work, and life in general. He emphasizes the importance of putting the effort into recovery. "When you have time off, is it really off?"

Recovery can be anything that gives you pleasure and peace while not activating your stress response: taking the kids for ice cream, cooking a meal with a partner, walking the dog, strolling through a park or the woods. These are all things that fit the bill, activities where there's no pressure, judgment, competition, or anxiety. Many people I work with, such as NBA coach Erik Spoelstra, are avid exercise buffs. "Everyone knows they need to give me that time [to work out], especially after a tough game," he says. "When I first started doing it, my staff kept interrupting me. I had to have a staff meeting to tell them to leave me alone during that time. I'm doing this so I can be better for you."

The best recovery tool is one we all have at our disposal: sleep. Unfortunately, while sleep comes easily for some people, it is more challenging for others. For those folks I like to recommend tart cherry juice, as in the juice from tart cherries, which are a different version of the fruit than the sweet cherries found in grocery stores. Tart cherries are bright red, as opposed to their deeper-hued, sweeter, ice-cream-making cousins, and are smaller and more sour. They are a good source of anthocyanins, which give them their pigmentation and are associated with anti-inflammatory and antioxidant benefits, as well as melatonin, a hormone that helps regulate sleep. Which helps explain the myriad of health benefits derived from them: reduced inflammation, muscle recovery, and (ta-da!) the duration and quality of sleep. This is why many Navy SEALs drink a few ounces of tart cherry juice before bed, as do many professional athletes.

If tart cherry juice is the sleep good guy, then its bad-guy nemesis is the smartphone, tablet, computer, or TV screen. The brain has something called the pineal gland, which takes its cues from light. Back before humans figured out how to create light, the setting of the sun activated the pineal gland, flooding the body with melatonin, a hormone associated with our natural circadian rhythm. It helps transition the body into sleep mode. Man-made light delays this process, but it is the "blue light" that emits from phones and these other screens that is the most egregious culprit. This light possesses a shorter wavelength and higher energy than other colors, which is great for boosting alertness and attention but a detriment when sleep is the objective.

If you are on your phone or laptop in the evening, you are essentially telling your brain that it is not time to sleep. For many people, it is folly to shut off the phone or TV, turn off the light, and expect sleep to come quickly. This isn't the way the body works. Try to give yourself at least an hour of screen-free time before turning out the lights, or at least turn your screen to night mode, which reduces blue light.

Many elite performers I've worked with use sensory deprivation tanks (a.k.a. float tanks) to recover. A float tank is an enclosed tank filled with a shallow pool of warm water that is saturated with salt, enabling people to effortlessly keep their eyes, nose, and mouth comfortably above the surface. The treatment is formally known as Floatation-REST (Reduced Environmental Stimulation Therapy). Float tanks were invented in the 1950s by researchers trying to understand how the brain responds to an environment completely lacking sensory input. They discovered that rather than falling asleep, people in such an environment stay fully awake and aware. This was an interesting outcome, but also somewhat of a problem, given that the original tanks were vertical and required participants to wear a cumbersome helmet so they could breathe. As a result, the float tank market was limited to only highly motivated individuals, such as NASA astronauts. Fortunately, the tanks have gone horizontal and gotten more spacious, and there are now hundreds of centers across the country.

Very few humans get to experience pure sensory deprivation. There's always something tickling the five senses. Even in utero, the fetus experiences sounds and physical movement. So depriving a person of all of that sensory input, which is what happens in a float tank, is an intense experience. What if I were to deprive you of all food and drink (except water) for a week? By the end of that time, you'd be hungry and uncomfortable (and angry at me!), but otherwise OK. If I were to then hand you an apple, you'd bite into it and immediately experience the most delicious apple you've ever eaten. Deprived of all food for a week, your taste buds would be hypersensitive to anything.

Float tanks achieve the same effect, but for the brain. Coming out of the float, where it is deprived of all sensory input for a period of time, the brain (and mind) is like those taste buds missing food for a week. It is hypersensitive to any input, creating an enhanced ability to think and focus. I've seen this work with many people, including Navy SEALs and Los Angeles Dodgers (both organizations use float tanks regularly). They have markedly improved focus for a few days after float sessions. SEALs shoot better, ballplayers see the ball better, executives see new solutions to old problems. (Total sensory deprivation can be intimidating. Most tanks offer the option of dim light and/or soft sounds to help newbies ease into the experience.)

Nature walks are another extremely beneficial way to recover. Most of us live in urban or suburban environments and spend the bulk of our waking hours indoors, so we are far removed from nature most of the time. A growing body of research draws a link between this separation and increased levels of mental illness. The more we are removed from nature, the more depressed and anxious we become. Conversely, returning to nature for even a short period of time—one to two hours—can have remarkable restorative effects. Numerous studies have confirmed this finding. A 2018 study showed that immersing oneself in nature has a stronger restorative effect than watching a nature video or working out.[2] A 2015 paper concludes that a ninety-minute walk in nature leads to a decrease in rumination, the usually harmful process of focusing on emotional causes and consequences, and decreased activity in a part of the brain (the subgenual prefrontal cortex) associated with sadness.[3] Nature walking improves the mood, calms racing thoughts, and reduces sadness. This isn't just some faddish guru suggestion; it's physiology at work.

Walking in nature is easy. You don't need to transport yourself deep into a national park or forest. In fact, you don't even need a forest; a local park or garden will do just fine. It does, though, require a bit of concentration. Put away the phone and resist the urge to pop in earbuds. Let all five senses attune themselves to the nature around them. Notice the sounds of the birds, see the plants and trees, feel the air on your face and the dirt underfoot. In a way, forest bathing is the opposite activity of float tanks, since it fully activates all five senses rather than shutting them down. The beneficial effects, though, are similar: renewed energy and increased focus.

Other recovery techniques I have seen work very well include yoga and meditation. Then there's Mike Dowdy's approach. The champion wakeboarder uses float tank sessions, sleep, and checking in with people he loves as recovery techniques, but he also advocates doing things he sucks at. "There's a new sport: wake foil-ing," Mike says. "The way you ride is very different; it's like flying a wing. I'm terrible at it! It's hard as shit! So I just leave the baggage at the door and be open-minded about it. I don't think about it or try too hard, just have fun." Trying something new like this gives Mike the chance to do something active while forgetting about the stresses of training and competition. He might not be giving his body a rest, but he's certainly giving his mind one.

Nathan Chen's guitar serves the same purpose. "In figure skat-ing I'm trying to achieve a version of excellence. When I do other things, like playing guitar, I'm not trying at all to be excellent. I can still work on getting better, but I don't get frustrated. I don't have the need to be the best guitarist." (I tried to reach Eric Clapton to see how figure skating helps him recover from being the world's best guitarist, but he hasn't gotten back to me yet.)

Finally, there's Erick Spoelstra's technique for helping his team recover from a tough stretch: gratitude. Practicing gratitude has all sorts of beneficial effects, including, according to one 2020 study, reduced depression, anxiety, and moderated stress response, so Eric is following the science.[4] "They come into the locker room [after a game or practice] and everyone is expecting us to beat them up. Instead, sometimes I'll get everyone to sit in a circle and ask them, what are you grateful about outside of this game? Or I'll ask them, how did you get here? Some of the best team meetings I've ever had are when guys just tell their story. I give them an exercise: when you leave here, contact two to three people that have really helped you. Then a week later, I'll ask them who those people were." Erik's approach boosts balance as well as recovery. The exercise reminds players of who they are outside of basketball and how much they have accomplished just to be there in the room, while giving them the space to recharge.

WELCOME TO WILLIAMS SONOMA

Several years into her CIA career, Patty Brandmaier's progress stalled. Her boss told her that her career as an analyst might be in jeopardy. This was a "find yourself" moment that proved a catalyst for Patty's future success. She considered what she valued, what she wanted to be known for, what she enjoyed, and where she wanted to have the most impact, and adjusted how she approached her job and life. From then on, through successes and setbacks, Patty always took time out to reflect on this experience and what she learned about herself and her values. "Every time I faltered it was because I lost sight of my goals and values. By coming back to them I regained my footing, with myself and others." Focusing on identity propelled her leadership growth, impact, and trajectory.

To help maintain that perspective, Patty decided she needed more balance in her life. Spending fewer hours at the agency and more time doing other things, she reasoned, might be helpful in keeping her in sync with those core goals and values. She loves to learn new things and to cook, so she got a job working evenings at Williams Sonoma, a retailer of luxury kitchen goods. She even helped them open a brand-new store. Besides working retail, Patty invested more time lifting weights at the local gym and biking. The new balance helped get her career back on track.

Balance, as in "work-life balance," has become a cliché. Nevertheless, it is critical to performance. A person who invests only in one or two aspects of their life is setting themselves up for subpar performance. This doesn't mean you have to pay attention every day (or even every week or every year) to all six of your life pillars. Reality dictates that many times you have to let some of those balls drop. But know that you are doing this, and figure out how to rebalance things in the future.

If you're not sure how to do this, stop by your local Williams Sonoma store and ask a friendly team member. She could just be a CIA officer.

LEARNED EXCELLENCE ACTION PLAN—BALANCE AND RECOVERY

OPTIMUM PERFORMANCE REQUIRES
BALANCE—INVESTING TIME AND
ENERGY ACROSS SIX ASPECTS OF
LIFE—AND RECOVERY—ALLOWING
TIME AND SPACE TO RECOVER AFTER
PERFORMANCE. TO PRACTICE THESE:

Give yourself permission to let the balls drop, underinvesting in some aspects of balance for days or weeks. But be aware of the situation, and plan to rectify it as soon as possible.

Give yourself the time and space to recover from performance. Sleep, exercise, gratitude, nature, float tanks, yoga, meditation, and doing things you suck at are all good techniques.

CHAPTER 8

Practicing Excellence

Most people have an inherent ability
which gets them to a certain point.
Beyond that, getting better has to be
learned.

— Nathan Chen, Olympic gold medalist and world
champion figure skater

The best performers in the world are not born excellent—they learn excellence. They practice the principles we have outlined in this book so they can get better at their craft every day. They start with deeply understanding their identity: What are their values? What motivates them? My clients codify this in their personal credo, which they use to help make decisions.

They set big goals across six aspects of their lives: work, relationships, health, spirituality, hobbies, and legacy. What do they want to be true in each of these areas in one, three, and six months? They develop action plans to bring those goals to fruition.

They select a mindset that will serve them best, with characteristics such as grit and growth that help them in their quest to constantly improve. They activate that mindset through the things they can control: their attitude, effort, and behavior. They stretch themselves to take on risks and sometimes fail, using those experiences as opportunities to practice their mindset. They adjust their mindset based on the different roles they play in life, since what creates excellence in one realm may be very different from what does so in another.

They prioritize process over outcome. They know that if they focus relentlessly on their process, the wins will come. They have the same twenty-four hours in their day as the rest of us, but they adopt practices to ensure they get the very most out of that time. They prize consistency, making changes methodically and only after consulting valid and vetted sources. When they alter some part of their process, they do so incrementally, seeing how it works rather than blowing everything up and starting over. They have an approach for turning failure into success.

They practice and employ techniques to help them manage their human stress response. These include visualization, contingency planning, self-awareness, 4444 breathing, pre- and post-performance routines, goal segmentation, countering fixed beliefs, black-boxing, unpacking the box after the event, and remembering their teammates. Understanding and practicing these techniques helps them stay calm and focused under the stress of performance.

They know how to maintain balance and give themselves the space to recover after performances. They invest in multiple aspects of their lives, not just the ones where they perform the most. When time and circumstances make this impossible, they are aware of the imbalance and have a plan to put things right. They actively practice recovery, using techniques that range from mundane (sleep, taking the kids to the park) to exotic (nature bathing, sensory deprivation tanks).

When I give talks on Learned Excellence to companies, teams, and other organizations, these are the principles I cover. By the conclusion of the talk, the audience is appreciative and curious. They almost always ask the same questions: How do I get started? What are the biggest barriers to learning excellence? How can I help my coworkers and teammates learn excellence? How can I teach excellence to my kids? (I hear that one the most.) And finally, I don't feel like I'm elite or a top performer; is this stuff applicable for me? Before we wrap up this book and I let you go, let's tackle these questions. Hint: the answer to the last one is YES!

THERE'S A LOT HERE! HOW DO I GET STARTED?

One of the biggest problems people have with achieving excellence is they focus on reputation rather than identity. So if you aren't sure where to start, understanding your identity is an excellent first step. Create your personal credo, following the steps in chapter 3, so that you have a foundation of values upon which to build your excellence. What you do, who you work with, and other external factors may change, but the foundation of who you are and who you aspire to be evolves very little. Invest the time to learn and understand it.

Then, set goals: short-, mid-, and long-term ones. The exact timing can vary, but I usually ask my clients to start with one, three, and six months. Establish these goals across the major aspects of your life (work and family are good places to start) and have an action plan for making good on them.

To achieve your goals, get more disciplined in how you manage your time. I suggest one approach in chapter 5; there are others that are equally effective. If adopting better time management practices is challenging, start small, maybe trying it for just a couple of days a week. See how it goes, then expand it until you get to the point where you are intentionally investing all of your waking hours in your priorities. This doesn't mean you have to be "on" or productive for all of those hours, simply that when you are goofing off you are doing so intentionally.

Create a feedback ecosystem. Who are the people that can give you the best input on your performance, have been vetted (they have your best interest in mind), and are valid (they know what they are talking about)? Identify these people, ask for their help, and schedule regular check-ins. Identify an accountability partner, someone who will help you keep tabs on your progress goals, and establish a regular cadence with that person as well.

How do you approach risk? Would you rather be more of a risk taker, or less of one? How do you handle failure? Or better, how do you want to handle it? What is the process you will use to learn from it and improve? Reflect on these points and write them down. How we approach risk and failure is core to our mindset, so taking inventory is a good place to start.

There are ten adversity tolerance techniques. Pick one of them—I usually recommend 4444 breathing—and practice it until it becomes second nature. Then pick another, and another.

So there's your getting-started to-do list. Too much? Then tackle them one at a time. Start with the first one, live it for a while, then move on to the next one. It doesn't much matter which one you choose, just that you choose one and get started. Remember Carli Lloyd, the women's soccer World Cup champion and Olympic gold medalist we first met in chapter 3? She fueled her rise to success by making lists and working at them. "If I couldn't do something, I would keep at it. The more you do something, it becomes a habit. I'd start chipping away and getting a little bit better every day," she says.

Be like Carli. Make a list and get after it.

The corollary to the getting started question is "What are the biggest barriers for people to learning excellence?" That one is easy: excuses. I don't know where to start. I don't have time. I'll get to it later. I'm not sure I can do this. You might have more creative ones. Excuses are a form of negative self-talk, so if you are hearing them in your head you already know your first step toward learning excellence: counter the negative self-talk and stop with the excuses. You *do* know where to start—I just told you. You *do* have time; in fact, doing this well creates time in your schedule. You shouldn't put it off, because when does it ever make sense to delay something that will make you healthier, happier, and more successful? And yes, you can do this. Anyone can.

HOW CAN I HELP MY COWORKERS AND TEAMMATES LEARN EXCELLENCE?

The pillars of Learned Excellence can apply to teams as well as individuals. This is a big component of leadership: How can I raise the excellence of my team? How can I help my colleagues and teammates (or team members) learn excellence, even those who may not be as motivated to do so?

Start by modeling excellence. Show the people around you what learning excellence looks like. Follow the principles I discuss in this book, but take the extra step of sharing what you are doing with others. Talk about your credo, share your goals with teammates, show how you treat failures as pivots, and help others practice 4444 breathing. Learning excellence is contagious, so sharing your practices and results with others may pique their curiosity to try it. Remember the simple mantras: know your credo, trust the process, control the controllables, black-box it. These make the principles more accessible and easier to remember.

Create an environment where it's OK to speak one's mind. Groupthink, where team members all vie to see who can agree the fastest with the leader, is failure mode for teams. Encourage all team members to bring their unique perspective and opinions to the fore as often as they can. A good technique for practicing this is the "after-action reviews" we covered earlier. After any important event, get together as a team to talk about what went well and what can be improved. One easy way to run an AAR is to use the phrase "one up, one to improve." What is one thing that went well? What is one thing we can do better? This is a handy little mantra that can quickly lead to honest conversation. The process of AARs is as important as the outcomes. It is critical that every team member feels like they can be open and honest in providing their feedback without fear of judgment or repercussion. This is especially helpful for newer members of the team, who are usually more hesitant to speak up in a new environment.

To further counter groupthink, many military and sports teams will assign a devil's advocate in meetings where important decisions are being discussed. It is this person's role to question the prevailing direction of the conversation, look for blind spots, and ask challenging questions. If everyone is leaning toward a decision, it is the devil's advocate's job to be forceful in questioning the wisdom of that decision. The military rotates the role among team members every meeting, so everyone gets a turn at being the dissenting voice.

Practice positive self-talk with the team. Organizations can be rigorous, demanding, and enervating; sometimes nothing feels good enough. So be the cheerleader for the team: reinforce what has been working, celebrate good news with exuberance, and try to close every day or week with optimism. Emotions are contagious, so practicing positivity within a team will rub off on others.

Understand team members' intrinsic motivators. Extrinsic motivators abound in most team environments. Most companies, for example, have performance review processes that periodically assign a grade to each team member, which dictates critical things like raises and promotions. People are held to KPIs (key performance indicators) that measure most aspects of what they do every day. In virtually every field, we are trained to create and track various metrics to tell us how well we are doing. So it is only natural that when discussing performance, it is these extrinsic factors that get all the attention.

It is just as natural that extrinsic factors only partially motivate high performance. Yes, you want to do well so you can get a good performance score or grade, which might lead to getting a raise or attending that great school. But you also want to do well because of how it makes you feel, how it aligns with your values, how you enjoy succeeding as a team, or how the work excites or inspires you. Extrinsic factors only go so far when it comes to motivating excellence. The intrinsic ones are what push us over the top. To get better performance from team members, learn more about their intrinsic motivators. What are their core values, what is their engine? Learning these things about your teammates, as well as yourself, can help create a deeper understanding of how to improve team performance.

Bob Reiff had a golden opportunity to help his team start to adapt Learned Excellence principles during the COVID pandemic in 2020 and 2021. I've been working with Bob since 2020. Bob was a senior vice president at Lincoln Financial in St. Louis at the time, and he brought me in to coach him and his team on learning to optimally perform during adversity. When the pandemic hit, Bob saw it as a good opportunity to observe, influence, and improve his team's approach to their work, in particular their mindset. He modeled and communicated how he wanted to focus on the controllables—attitude, effort, behavior—frequently reminding them to stay in the circle. He coached them on seeing failure as an opportunity to learn and adapt, and developed training programs using Learned Excellence principles. He shared his practices of visualization and positive self-talk, which he first learned as a high school football player, with his leaders and team members. He encouraged sleep, nutrition, and exercise. He spent more time listening, and urged his leadership team to do the same, which helped them develop a more holistic understanding of their team members' lives and motivators.

The results were mostly great. "I was very impressed by their resilience," he recalls. "A lot of people found themselves during the pandemic. They questioned how they were approaching their business, how they were going to market. I saw a lot of self-assessment—they got better at constantly asking themselves how they could get better." Not everyone thrived, though. Bob had some people who weren't as resourceful and had a hard time adapting to the new norms of business. But these were a minority. Overall, Bob found that when he modeled and communicated his principles of excellence, his team learned and thrived.

HOW CAN I TEACH EXCELLENCE TO MY KIDS?

I hear this question more often than any other. Parents always want the best for their kids, of course, but the sense I get from the people asking this question (and from being a parent of two myself) is that the world in which we are raising kids today is more fraught than ever, and parents are looking for help. The upcoming generation consists of digital natives, having never lived in a world without raucous social media, infinite streaming video, and the world's information at their fingertips. Blessing? Curse? One can argue both sides, but there's no doubt it's the reality that parents and their kids must navigate. How can they instill the principles of excellence in their kids amid this loud, digital world?

Derrick Walker has a smart approach. Derrick is the former minor-league baseball player and Navy SEAL candidate who is now a Nike business leader. In addition to forging this interesting career, Derrick and his wife have found the time to have eight children. Derrick notes with pride that while there is a fair amount of chaos in his home ("we're good at playing zone defense"), he and his wife lead with love and compassion and have successfully guided his children through many challenges. His secret? Failure. "Most of my development came as a result of failure," Derrick says. "Parents need to let their kids go along their journey and give them opportunities to fail. We encourage them to put themselves in situations where they might fail. Failure isn't inevitable, but there are a lot of situations growing up that present setbacks and disappointments. My job is to help them fail forward, and walk with them through the journey."

Peter Naschak, the retired Navy SEAL, is another proponent of pushing kids to take risks. Peter was raised by a single mom from a young age; it was part of her nature to put her kids into situations where they might fail. "She wouldn't let us bitch our way out of something we didn't want to do," Peter says. "She'd tell us, let's try it and see what happens." He recalls a family trip to Hawaii when he was about nine years old. "We were watching some guys diving off cliffs into the water. I really wanted to try it, but I was scared. Mom could see that I wanted to try it, so she encouraged me to ask one of the divers for help. I was more scared of talking to a stranger than I was of diving. So she said, 'We're not leaving until you ask one of them.'" Peter eventually approached one of the divers, and with his help was soon happily diving into the water from the rocks. "She put me in those situations a lot [asking for help from strangers, I presume, not cliff diving]. That gave me more tools than if she had controlled things more."

This approach of pushing kids is consistent across all of the performers with whom I work. Their number one piece of advice for parents is to put kids in challenging situations, where they have ample opportunity to succeed but also to fail. The consensus is that the next generation is more risk averse than their predecessors, perhaps shaped by the fear of reputational damage in an era of social media. To counter this, parents should encourage their kids to take risks. That way they can experience "micro failures," instances where things may not go as planned but the consequences are relatively minor. They discover their resilience and develop a more healthy attitude toward risk.

Marcus Luttrell, the retired SEAL, makes it a goal to tell his kids at least three times per day that he loves them. But he also says, "If you don't put stress on a kid, life will. Axe [his son] tells me all the time I force him to do things against his will. I tell him, he wouldn't try if I didn't force him."

Another Derrick Walker parenting tip employs a simple coaching technique: questioning and listening. "We try to ask them thought-provoking questions," Derrick says. "Why did you do that? Is there another way to think about that? Is the thought process the most beneficial one? How can you think differently? Sometimes they expect me to say something, and I don't. I leave it ambiguous so they have to think it through a bit."

The open form of inquiry espoused by Derrick is another common theme among my performer parents. Steve Pitts, the former Reno chief of police, has three grandkids. He loves to ask them questions, even when he knows the answer. "The best thing you can do is talk to them and ask questions. They start self-checking, even reflecting at that young age. When they ask me things, I turn it back around. Why did you ask me that?" This light verbal jousting is a form of failure in itself. When kids venture to answer a question they don't know, they are taking a risk. If they get it wrong (fail), they will learn from that experience and try again.

My wife and I have two children, both of whom are well on their way to becoming caring, interesting, successful adults. Like Derrick and Steve, we liked to ask our kids questions when they were younger. We called it the "why game," asking them questions that usually flow the other way in the typical parent-child relationship: Why is the sky blue? Why do fish have scales? Why are flowers so brightly colored? The answer—the what—is irrelevant. It's the process of reasoning—the how and why—that matters. (Again, focus on process, not outcomes.) Perhaps the reason I enjoyed this game so much was that much of my education revolved around mass regurgitation of facts, which was all about the what and not the how and why. My wife and I wanted to avoid this with our kids. The why game helped us raise more curious people who aren't afraid to work things out if they don't know the answers.

Negative self-talk starts early, so many of the parents with whom I work keep an eye out for it. Insurance executive Ted Brown listens for negative self-talk around the dinner table. He has a mantra with one of his children who is especially prone to self-doubt. "I tell him daily, you're a good kid, you're a good person," Ted says. "I make him repeat it. Then I tell him, you are going to be able to work through any challenges life throws at you, and I make him repeat that, too." These are mantras that will turn into beliefs, and stick with the young man throughout his life.

Push kids out of their comfort zone. Encourage them to take risks so they can practice how to learn and recover from failure; trial and learn, not trial and error. Ask them questions and don't tell them the answers; let them figure them out for themselves.

Listen for negative self-talk and teach them how to replace it with positive.

All of this can usually be accomplished with a few simple questions.

"Why?" Gets them in the habit of resilient thinking, working things out and not being stymied when they don't get it right the first time.

"What did you learn today that you didn't know yesterday?" Helps foster curiosity and learning.

"Were you brave?" Reminds them to push outside their comfort zone.

Finally, "Were you kind, especially to yourself?" Because kindness breeds resilience.

I DON'T FEEL LIKE I'M ELITE OR A TOP PERFORMER . . . IS THIS STUFF APPLICABLE FOR ME?

Think of a performer you admire. It could be an entertainer, an athlete, an academic, a business, political, or community leader, a hero. Are you thinking of this person? Have a picture in your mind, maybe a song of theirs you can hum along to? Now, I guarantee you that person had to learn how to be excellent. They may have some remarkable abilities with which they were naturally blessed, but the mental aspects of excellence, their software, the stuff that makes them the best? They had to learn those. It may have been a natural process, as they absorbed best practices from parents, teachers, mentors, coaches, and friends. It may also be the result of a deliberate effort, as is the case with the many performers I have worked with. But one thing it is not: innate. The mental skills of high performance are not genetic or built into us. Which means anyone can learn them. Anyone.

So what if you aren't elite in your field, a so-called top performer? Most people aren't. But you are still a performer. Not in the sense that you are putting on a show, but in the real sense of performance, the one where you derive pleasure and satisfaction from doing your best, where you make a difference, and where you care what happens. You perform at your job and in your classes. You perform as a child, parent, sibling, and relative. You perform in your church and community. You perform as an athlete, whether you run ultramarathons or just like a walk to the corner and back. You perform as a friend. You perform as a partner. You perform.

In each of these realms, you can perform better. You can take the principles I set forth in this book, learn and practice them, and build them into your daily habits. You can improve every day, constantly learning about yourself and your environment. You can see that this is easier than you think, and a lot of fun. You can.

Maybe you still have that nagging feeling: I'm not really a performer, and all this stuff seems like a lot of work. Or, I don't care about getting better, I'm fine with the way things are. Leave me alone.

No, I will not leave you alone! Because I believe that the skills of high performance are within the reach of every single person, that they are simple to learn and straightforward to practice. I also believe, because I have seen it thousands of times, that fulfilling potential feels great. Don't believe me? Try it. Learn excellence, just for a week, and see how it goes. Watch how it turns into another week, a month, a year, a way of life. See how you do better at work and school, at home, in your community and relationships. Feel how good that feels. Nice, right? You're not there yet, but you will be.

American historian, writer, and philosopher Will Durant wrote, "We are what we repeatedly do. Excellence, then, is not an act, but a habit."[1] Make it yours. Learning excellence starts now.

LEARNED EXCELLENCE ACTION PLANS

Sample 30-Day, 90-Day, and 180-Day Plans
Use these sample templates to help get started with a Learned
Excellence Action Plan.

30-Day Learned Excellence Action Plan	Date Completed
Create your 10-word personal credo (identity markers/values) within the next 10 days.	
Identify, write down, and verbally share one goal with a friend, coworker, or coach in the following 6 pillars: work, relationships, health, spirituality, hobby, legacy.	
Identify 4 to 6 people who can be vetted and valid feedback nodes for you. Ensure they are people who can give you trusted feedback.	
Eliminate the "blank space" in your calendar 2 days per week and color-code those 2 days of tasks with red, yellow, or green.	

30-Day Learned Excellence Action Plan	Date Completed
Practice 4444 (4 seconds in, 4–6 seconds out, 4 minutes, 4 times per day) 3 days per week. (Remember: 6 breaths per minute is the key.)	
Identify your top 4 roles (worker, parent, significant other, etc.) and choose 3 words you think your mindset needs to be within each of those roles.	
Develop a performance routine to help transition in/out of each of those roles (mantra, word reminders on your phone, music, meditation).	
As part of your bedtime routine, visualize (with as many senses as possible and for about 3 minutes) something that went well for you that day—do this 4 times per week.	
Sign up for a float tank session or yoga class, or start a gratitude journal—documenting the things you are grateful for and looking at/adding to it 3 times per week.	

90-Day Learned Excellence Action Plan	Date Completed
Educate someone about what it means to "stay in the circle." Attitude, effort, and behavior are the only things you control. Teaching it means you know it.	
Identify, write down, and verbally share 2 goals with a friend, coworker, or coach in the following 6 pillars: work, relationships, health, spirituality, hobby, legacy.	
Push yourself to get out of your comfort zone at least one time per week (volunteer for a project, ask more questions, new workout/hobby, dating, ask for feedback).	
Eliminate the "blank space" in your calendar 4 days per week and color-code those 4 days of tasks with red, yellow, or green.	
Practice 4444 (4 seconds in, 4–6 seconds out, 4 minutes, 4 times per day) 5 days per week. (Remember: 6 breaths per minute is the key.)	

90-Day Learned Excellence Action Plan	Date Completed
Practice visualizing before a big performance (sporting event, presentation, client meeting, date, team meeting) the night before and 1 to 3 hours before the event.	
Develop contingency plans before each of your major performances/events (various plans to fall back on if something happens, responses to various questions, etc.).	
Monitor/track the number of hours of sleep you're averaging nightly. Attempt to get between 7 to 9 hours of sleep at least 6 days per week.	
Practice positive self-talk and examine your belief system. Check in weekly and look for the evidence when negative thoughts occur (challenge irrational thoughts).	

180-Day Learned Excellence Action Plan	Date Completed
Reexamine your personal credo (10 words of identity markers/values) and determine if there are words you'd like to add/remove.	
Challenge and remind yourself to be more "challenge" vs. "threat" mindset oriented (with accompanying self-talk) when obstacles happen. Keep count of how many times your mindset is challenge ("it's nothing more than a challenge") rather than threat ("my reputation, my ego, judgment"). Goal is 80 percent challenge statements.	
Get into the habit of only making one change to a process at a time. Then measure the results. Changing too much too soon is a haphazard method to improve.	
Eliminate the "white space" in your calendar 6 days per week and color-code those 6 days of tasks with red, yellow, or green.	
Practice 4444 (4 seconds in, 4–6 seconds out, 4 minutes, 4 times per day) 5 days per week. (Remember: 6 breaths per minute is the key.)	

180-Day Learned Excellence Action Plan	Date Completed
Set 2 larger goals in each of 3 areas (work, relationship, health) and segment those goals into smaller, manageable pieces. Set a 6-month goal in each of those areas and segment each of them into 1-month smaller-piece goals using the SMART acronym. Measure those smaller goals being met monthly.	
Practice "black-boxing" miscues, mistakes, and errors and staying "mission-minded" until the end of the performance. Then unpack the "box" and learn from the errors.	
Do a monthly self-awareness check-in (color-coded green, yellow, and red) in the following areas: life events, stress, mood, sleep, health, substance use, concentration, and workplace climate). If you have a yellow or red, develop a plan to address those "mental performance vital sign" areas. Do it so they don't affect performance.	
Build "technology" breaks or blackout blocks (emails, phones/texts, social media) into your daily schedule (even committed short breaks are beneficial).	

ACKNOWLEDGMENTS

This book would not have been possible without the participation of the fabulous performers listed below. Each of these wonderful people gave us their time and support, all of them with the same energy and passion that helped them become the best in their craft. Thank you very, very much:

- Alex Krongard, retired Navy SEAL admiral, former National Security Council staff
- Alex Myers, professional esport athlete
- Andy Walshe, former head of Human Performance for Red Bull, former high performance director, US Ski and Snowboard Team
- Anthony Oshinuga, professional aerobatics pilot
- Ben Potvin, former Cirque du Soleil artist, head coach, and performance designer
- Blaine Vess, entrepreneur, investor, philanthropist
- Bob Reiff, business executive and leader
- Carli Lloyd, US Women's national soccer team, two-time FIFA World Cup champion, two-time Olympic gold medalist, two-time FIFA player of the year

- David Colturi, former US National 10m Diving and Red Bull Cliff Diving champion
- David Wurtzel, two-time Firefighter Challenge world champion (2017, 2018)
- Deena Ryerson, senior assistant attorney general at Oregon Department of Justice
- Derrick Walker, finance leader at Nike, former baseball player and Navy SEAL candidate
- Erik Spoelstra, head coach, Miami Heat NBA team, two-time NBA champion
- Ian Walsh, professional big wave surfer
- Jim Lindell, retired Navy SEAL master chief, sniper for Captain Phillips Somali hostage rescue operation
- John Marx, retired police officer and hostage negotiator
- Joseph Maroon, neurosurgeon, Triathlete/Ironman, Pittsburgh Steelers physician
- Katy Stanfill, former Navy helicopter pilot, naval officer, US Naval Academy athlete
- Marcus Luttrell, retired Navy SEAL, "Lone Survivor" of Operation Red Wings
- Michael Dauro, former Navy SEAL platoon commander/leader
- Mike Dowdy, professional wakeboard rider, 2016 World Champion
- Nathan Chen, 2022 Men's Figure Skating Olympic gold medalist, three-time world champion, six-time US national champion
- Patty Brandmaier, former CIA analyst and senior leader
- Penelope Parmes, three-time world champion ballroom dancer, retired attorney

- Pete Naschak, retired Navy Command master chief, SEAL Team 5
- Rich Hill, Major League Baseball pitcher
- Steve Idoux, producer/president, Lockton Dallas
- Steve Pitts, former chief of police, Reno, Nevada
- Ted Brown, producer/president, Lockton Denver
- Tim Murphy, former US member of Congress (Pennsylvania), 2003–17
- Toby Miller, professional snowboarder
- Victor Zhang, chief investment officer, American Century Investments

I'd like to thank my wife, Andrea, and my two children, Lauren and Bryce, for their tireless love, support, and encouragement throughout the years. I'm proudest of my roles as a husband and father. The keys to our family unit have always been communication, trust, respect, compromise, curiosity, and fun. It has made everything easy and our home truly a sanctuary. You are the foundation and are always pushing me to further embrace my passion for helping others meet their potential. The best team I've ever been a part of is my family. Family is always first and my work is only possible because of your love and enthusiasm. What a fantastic journey it's been!

An enormous thank-you to my parents, Georges and Susie. My values, work ethic, and passion all started with you. This book and my career would not have happened without your early and constant support and direction.

I have a special ecosystem of dear friends—almost like my personal board of directors. The chairman of that board is my closest friend, Steve Godfrey. You deserve a huge thank-you! You're one of the most reflective and compassionate thinkers I know. Whether it was letting me bounce ideas off you, twisting my arm to take more time off to ski, hike, or bike, or using humor to take my mind off work, your friendship has been instrumental to keeping me balanced so I could complete this book.

I'd like to thank my mentors, Dr. William Perry and Dr. Jim Bauman. Bill was my dissertation chair and pushed me to set and meet high standards, to become both a good clinician and researcher, and to understand that the harder and less-traveled path is always the one worth taking. Jim is one of the best sport psychologists I've ever known and expertly mentored me as I transitioned into the work with professional sport. I've never seen anyone connect with athletes better. You have the trifecta: relatability, patience, and brilliance. Thank you both for making me a better professional and person.

A special thank-you to the members of the US military, and especially the members of US Special Operations. Within that group, a specific heartfelt thank-you to the US Navy SEALs and their families. Being the active-duty performance and clinical psychologist for this group of incredible human beings will always be the most relevant, meaningful, and important work of my professional life. Most people will never understand the daily sacrifices you make for our nation and those who need it most in the world. During my ten years with the SEALs, you taught me so much. You are all the pinnacle of human performance, especially in the mental toughness domain. And a special thank-you to the spouses and families of the Special Operations community. Your constant sacrifice (deployments, not knowing the details of your spouse's almost daily missions and operations, etc.) and your ability to navigate this sacrifice with perseverance, conviction, resourcefulness, and resilience is a superpower if there ever was one. It was an honor to work with these special warriors and to get to know their families. I'll always be loyal to Naval Special Warfare and just a phone call away—anytime, anywhere.

Thank you to all first responders. I have dear friends who are both police officers and firefighters and have spent the last decade presenting to dozens of police and fire departments, conferences, and summits with the goal of both learning from them and helping them improve resilience and excellence. I'm in constant awe of both who you are and what you do! Not many humans choose a life where they run toward danger. Each of you is a gift to your community. Thank you.

Thank you to the Los Angeles Dodgers, and most specifically Stan Kastan, Andrew Friedman, Josh Byrnes, Billy Gasparino, and Dave Roberts. When you hired me in 2016, you empowered me to build the mental performance assessment, selection, development, and optimization programs. I appreciate you allowing me to grow, spend more time with my family, and focus in latter years on the draft, scouting, and talent acquisition. For many years I've said, "In order to forge the best swords, you need the right steel." Also, a special thank-you to the late Tommy Lasorda. I'll always smile when I think of our many meals together and your fantastic stories about everything from game memories to the restaurants with the best pasta. The Dodgers organization embodies pure class, innovation, and sustained excellence, and you've all been a true highlight in my professional career.

Thank you to the Defense Office of Prepublication and Security Review. Within that office, Doug McComb and Paul Jacobsmeyer were extremely professional and thorough in reviewing the manuscript to ensure protection against the release of nonpublic information. Both of you were helpful and made the process painless. Your regular communication and amendments were sincerely appreciated.

Thank you to the Central Intelligence Agency's Prepublication Classification Review Board for reviewing interview excerpts and anecdotes within our manuscript. Your fast and precise turnaround was impressive and allowed us to meet our deadlines.

Thank you, Marina Krakovsky, our researcher, who enriched us with her curiosity and findings, pushed us with her comments and questions, and made us better with her editing suggestions. Until the next book, Marina!

Thank you to our editor, Hollis Heimbouch, who is not only a fine sounding board and wicked wordsmith, but a marathon runner and triathlete. When Hollis told us that as a performer she appreciated our material, we knew we were on to something. And thank you to our peerless agent, Jim Levine, who connected us with Hollis and took some of our calls while he practiced excellence walking the streets of New York City.

Finally, thank you to the thousands of other performers—military personnel, athletes, businesspeople, congressional representatives, lawyers, artists, human performance leaders, and medical professionals—I have had the pleasure to work with over the course of my career, both as clients and colleagues. It has been an honor.

NOTES

Chapter 1: You the Performer

1. Self-determination theory, backed by a large body of research, posits that competence is one of three innate psychological needs (along with autonomy and relatedness) that contribute to our wellness. Richard M. Ryan and Edward L. Deci, "Self-Determination Theory and the Facilitation of Intrinsic Motivation, Social Development, and Well-Being," *American Psychologist* 55, no. 1 (January 2000): 68–78, https://doi.org/10.1037/0003-066X.55.1.68.

2. Nancy E. Newall et al., "Regret in Later Life: Exploring Relationships Between Regret Frequency, Secondary Interpretive Control Beliefs, and Health in Older Individuals," *International Journal of Aging and Human Development* 68, no. 4 (2009): 261–88, https://doi.org/10.2190/AG.68.4.a.

Chapter 2: Learning About Excellence

1. Martin J. Barwood et al., "Breath-Hold Performance During Cold Water Immersion: Effects of Psychological Skill Training," *Aviation, Space, and Environmental Medicine* 77, no. 11 (November 2006): 1136–42, https://www.researchgate.net/publication/6709881_Breath-hold_performance_during_cold_water_immersion_Effects_of_psychological_skills_training.

2. Garvey, Hershiser, and Yeager helped anchor several great Dodger teams in the 1970s and '80s. Lasorda managed the team from 1976 until 1996.

Chapter 3: Values and Goals

1. This quote is probably apocryphal, but let's not go down that road. Garson O'Toole, "When You Come to a Fork in the Road, Take It," Quote Investigator, accessed March 13, 2023, https://quoteinvestigator.com/2013/07/25/fork-road/#google_vignette.

2. A 2000 study in the *Journal of Personality and Social Psychology* contains a summary of previous research into how past events and resulting beliefs

influence current behavior. The paper starts by noting, "People who have behaved in a certain way at one point in time are likely to do so again," citing several studies that support the statement. D. Albarracin and R. S. Wyer Jr., "The Cognitive Impact of Past Behavior: Influences on Beliefs, Attitudes, and Future Behavioral Decisions," *Journal of Personality and Social Psychology* 79, no. 1 (2000): 5–22, https://doi.org/10.1037/0022-3514.79.1.5.

Chapter 4: Mindset

1. "Google Books Ngram Viewer for Term 'Mindset,'" Google Books, accessed March 13, 2023, https://books.google.com/ngrams/graph?content =mindset&year_start=1800&year_end=2019&corpus=26&smoothing=3 &direct_url=t1%3B%2Cmindset%3B%2Cc0#t1%3B%2Cmindset%3B %2Cc0.

2. "Google Trends Explore for Term 'Mindset,'" Google Trends, accessed March 13, 2023, https://trends.google.com/trends/explore?date=all&q=mindset.

3. "Bewusstseinslage," *APA Dictionary of Psychology*, American Psychological Association, accessed March 13, 2023, https://dictionary.apa.org /bewusstseinslage.

4. Alia J. Crum, Peter Salovey, and Shawn Achor, "Rethinking Stress: The Role of Mindsets in Determining the Stress Response," *Journal of Personality and Social Psychology* 104, no. 4 (2013): 716–33, https://doi.org/10.1037 /a0031201.

5. Matt Abrahams, "Mindset Matters: How to Embrace the Benefits of Stress," Stanford Graduate School of Business, accessed March 13, 2023, https:// www.gsb.stanford.edu/insights/mindset-matters-how-embrace-benefits -stress.

6. Christopher J. Beedie and Abigail J. Foad, "The Placebo Effect in Sports Performance: A Brief Review," *Sports Medicine* 39, no. 4 (2009): 313–29, https://doi.org/0112-1642/09/0004-0313.

7. Lysann Damisch, Barbara Stoberock, and Thomas Mussweiler, "Keep Your Fingers Crossed! How Superstition Improves Performance," *Psychological Science* 21, no. 7 (May 28, 2010): 1014–20, https://doi.org /10.1177/0956797610372631.

8. Wayne Dollard, "How Pickleball Really Got Its Name!," *Pickleball Magazine*, January 2021, https://www.pickleballmagazine.com/pickleball-articles /How-Pickleball-Really-Got-Its-Name!

9. Not coincidentally, one of the earliest examples of the study of the mental aspect of sports performance is the iconic 1974 bestseller *The Inner Game of Tennis*, by W. Timothy Gallwey (New York: Random House, 1974). Al-

though it doesn't use the term *mindset*, the book is all about how a stronger mental game directly affects outcome.

10. Carol Dweck, "What Having a Growth Mindset Actually Means," *Harvard Business Review*, January 13, 2016, https://hbr.org/2016/01/what-having-a -growth-mindset-actually-means.

11. Emily G. Liquin and Alison Gopnik, "Children Are More Exploratory and Learn More Than Adults in an Approach-Avoid Task," *Cognition* 218 (2022): 104940, https://doi.org/10.1016/j.cognition.2021.104940.

12. E. A. Gunderson et al., "Parent Praise to Toddlers Predicts Fourth Grade Academic Achievement Via Children's Incremental Mindsets," *Developmental Psychology* 54, no. 3 (2018): 397–409, https://doi.org/10.1037/dev0000444.

13. Daeun Park et al., "The Development of Grit and Growth Mindset During Adolescence," *Journal of Experimental Child Psychology* 198 (October 2020): 104889, https://doi.org/10.1016/j.jecp.2020.104889.

14. Adam M. Grant and Barry Schwartz, "Too Much of a Good Thing: The Challenge and Opportunity of the Inverted U," *Perspectives on Psychological Science* 6, no. 1 (2011): 61–76, https://doi.org/10.1177/1745691610393523.

15. David Tod, James Hardy, and Emily Oliver, "Effects of Self-Talk: A Systematic Review," *Journal of Sport and Exercise Psychology* 33, no. 5 (2011): 666–87, https://doi.org/10.1123/jsep.33.5.666.

16. E. Cross and O. Ayduk, "Self-Distancing: Theory, Research, and Current Directions," *Advances in Experimental Social Psychology* 55 (2017): 81–136, https://doi.org/10.1016/bs.aesp.2016.10.002.

17. James Hardy, Aled V. Thomas, and Anthony W. Blanchfield, "To Me, to You: How You Say Things Matters for Endurance Performance," *Journal of Sports Sciences* 37, no. 18 (2019): 2122–30, https://doi.org/10.1080/02640414 .2019.1622240.

18. Numerous studies confirm the effectiveness of pre-performance routines. This 2021 meta-study provides a good summary of them. Anton G. O. Rupprecht, Ulrich S. Tran, and Peter Gröpel, "The Effectiveness of Pre-Performance Routines in Sports: A Meta-Analysis," *International Review of Sport and Exercise Psychology* (October 2021), https://doi.org/10.1080 /1750984X.2021.1944271.

19. The researchers analyzed 2.5 million putts attempted by 421 golfers in 239 tournaments between 2004 and 2009. To get the data, the PGA mounted lasers around each hole of a course to measure and record within an inch the coordinates of each ball after every shot.

20. Devin G. Pope and Maurice E. Schweitzer, "Is Tiger Woods Loss Averse? Persistent Bias in the Face of Experience, Competition, and High Stakes,"

American Economic Review 101, no. 1 (2001): 12957, http://dx.doi.org /10.1257/aer.101.1.129.

21. Ryan Elmore and Andrew Urbaczewski, "Loss Aversion in Professional Golf," *Journal of Sports Economics* 22, no. 2 (2021): 202–17, https://doi.org /10.1177/1527002520967403.

Chapter 5: Process

1. Brad Aeon and Herman Aguinas, "It's About Time: New Perspectives and Insights on Time Management," *Academy of Management Perspectives* 31, no. 4 (2017): 309–30, https://doi.org/10.5465/amp.2016.0166.

2. Jonathan Baron and John C. Hershey, "Outcome Bias in Decision Evaluation," *Journal of Personality and Social Psychology* 54, no. 4 (1988): 569–57, http://bear .warrington.ufl.edu/brenner/mar7588/Papers/baron-hershey-jpsp1988.pdf.

3. Amos Tversky and Daniel Kahneman, "Availability: A Heuristic for Judging Frequency and Probability," *Cognitive Psychology* 5 (1973): 207–32, https:// familyvest.com/wp-content/uploads/2019/02/TverskyKahneman73.pdf.

4. Robert B. Durand, Fernando, M. Patterson, and Corey A. Shank, "Behavioral Biases in the NFL Gambling Market: Overreaction to News and the Recency Bias," *Journal of Behavioral and Experimental Finance* 31 (September 2021): 100522, https://doi.org/10.1016/j.jbef.2021.100522.

5. Michael Bar-Eli et al., "Action Bias Among Elite Soccer Goalkeepers: The Case of Penalty Kicks," *Journal of Economic Psychology* 28, no. 5 (2007): 606–21, https://doi.org/10.1016/j.joep.2006.12.001.

6. Peter Jensen Brown, "The History and Origin of 'Monday Morning Quarterback,'" *Early Sports and Pop Culture History Blog*, accessed March 13, 2023, https://esnpc.blogspot.com/2014/07/the-history-and-origin-of-monday.html.

Chapter 6: Adversity Tolerance

1. D. Meichenbaum and R. Cameron, "Stress Inoculation Training," in *Stress Reduction and Prevention*, ed. D. Meichenbaum and M. E. Jarenko (Boston: Springer, 1989), 115–54, https://doi.org/10.1007/978-1-4899-0408-9_5.

2. Research shows that while everyone is subject to fight, flight, or freeze, women also are prone to "tend and befriend" instincts when exposed to stressors, that is, keeping offspring safe (tend) and affiliating and seeking safety with others (befriend). Shelley E. Taylor et al., "Biobehavioral Responses to Stress in Females: Tend-and-Befriend, Not Fight-or-Flight," *Psychological Review* 107, no. 3 (2000): 411–29, https://doi.org/10.1037//0033-295X.107.3.411.

3. Robert M. Sapolsky, *Why Zebras Don't Get Ulcers*, 3rd ed. (New York: Holt Paperbacks, 2004), 11.

4. Sapolsky, *Why Zebras Don't Get Ulcers*, 6.

5. For example, a 2015 paper on KMI cites previous studies showing how the "frequency of KMI use increases with competitive level, differentiates professional players from amateurs, and distinguishes successful from unsuccessful Olympic track-and-field contenders." K. Richard Ridderinkhof and Marcel Brass, "How Kinesthetic Motor Imagery Works: A Predictive-Processing Theory of Visualization in Sports and Motor Expertise," *Journal of Physiology Paris* 109, nos. 1–3 (2015): 53–63, https://doi.org/10.1016/j.jphysparis.2015.02.003.

6. Paul S. Holmes and David J. Collins, "The PETTLEP Approach to Motor Imagery: A Functional Equivalence Model for Sport Psychologists," *Journal of Applied Sport Psychology* 13, no. 1 (2001): 60–83, https://doi.org/10.1080/10413200109339004.

7. A few studies in support of these points:

   A 2017 study in *Frontiers in Psychology* found that participants who practiced deep breathing (4 BPM in this study) had significantly better attention and lowered cortisol rates (an indicator of stress). Xiao Ma et al., "The Effect of Diaphragmatic Breathing on Attention, Negative Affect, and Stress in Healthy Adults," *Frontiers in Psychology* 8 (June 6, 2017): 874, https://doi.org/10.3389/fpsyg.2017.00874.

   A 2017 study of competitive shooters found that higher HRV is correlated with self-efficacy (confidence) and is a strong predictor of performance. E. Ortega and C. J. K. Wang, "Pre-Performance Physiological State: Heart Rate Variability as a Predictor of Shooting Performance," *Applied Psychophysiology and Biofeedback* 43, no. 1 (March 2018): 75–85, https://doi.org/10.1007/s10484-017-9386-9.

   Another 2017 study showed that breathing at 6 BPM for fifteen minutes improves mood, lowers blood pressure, and raises HRV. Patrick R. Steffen et al., "The Impact of Resonance Frequency Breathing on Measures of Heart Rate Variability, Blood Pressure, and Mood," *Frontiers in Public Health* 5 (August 25, 2017): 222, https://doi.org/10.3389/fpubh.2017.00222.

8. Szu-chi Huang, Liyin Jin, and Ying Zhang, "Step by Step: Sub-Goals as a Source of Motivation," *Organizational Behavior and Human Decision Processes* 141 (July 2017): 1–15, https://doi.org/10.1016/j.obhdp.2017.05.001.

9. L. Houser-Marko and K. M. Sheldon, "Eyes on the Prize or Nose to the Grindstone? The Effects of Level of Goal Evaluation on Mood and Motivation," *Personality and Social Psychology Bulletin* 34, no. 11 (2008): 1556–69, https://doi.org/10.1177/0146167208322618.

10. Dr. Ellis, who passed away in 2007, developed the ABC model in the mid-1950s as the cornerstone to a new therapeutic approach to mental health, which he called Rational Emotive Therapy. RET (now often called REBT, to include behavior) was one of the first examples of Cognitive Behavior Therapy (CBT), whereby a patient (usually with the aid of a therapist) examines and adjusts how they think about and approach things in an effort to improve mental health (primarily anxiety and depression). It was a distinctly different approach from the commonly accepted form of psychotherapy in practice at the time, in which a therapist helps the patient explore conscious and unconscious thoughts, emotions, and experiences from childhood as a way to explain and address mental health issues.

11. Shakespeare, *Hamlet*, 2.2.239–40.

12. Alia J. Crum, Peter Salovey, and Shawn Achor, "Rethinking Stress: The Role of Mindsets in Determining the Stress Response," *Journal of Personality and Social Psychology* 104, no. 4 (2013): 716–33, https://doi.org/10.1037/a0031201.

13. Kelly McGonigal, *The Upside of Stress: Why Stress Is Good for You, and How to Get Good at It* (New York: Avery, 2016), xxi.

Chapter 7: Balance and Recovery

1. Jarrod M. Haar et al., "Outcomes of Work-Life Balance on Job Satisfaction, Life Satisfaction, and Mental Health: A Study Across Seven Cultures," *Journal of Vocational Behavior* 85, no. 3 (December 2014): 361–73, https://doi.org/10.1016/j.jvb.2014.08.010.

2. Gunnthora Olafsdottir et al., "Health Benefits of Walking in Nature: A Randomized Controlled Study Under Conditions of Real-Life Stress," *Environment and Behavior* 52, no. 3 (2018): 248–74, https://doi.org/10.1177/0013916518800798.

3. Gregory N. Bratman et al., "Nature Experience Reduces Rumination and Subgenual Prefrontal Cortex Activation," *Proceedings of the National Academy of Sciences* 112, no. 28 (June 29, 2015), https://doi.org/10.1073/pnas.1510459112.

4. Lilian Jans-Beken et al., "Gratitude and Health: An Updated Review," *Journal of Positive Psychology* 15, no. 6 (2020): 743–82, https://doi.org/10.1080/17439760.2019.1651888.

Chapter 8: Practicing Excellence

1. Will Durant, *The Story of Philosophy: The Lives and Opinions of the Greater Philosophers* (New York: Simon & Schuster, 1926), 69.

INDEX

ABOUT THE AUTHORS

Eric Potterat, PhD, is a clinical and performance psychologist and a leading expert in individual and organizational performance optimization. Eric retired as a commander from the US Navy after twenty years of service, the last ten of which he spent as the psychologist for the Navy SEALs. He has been credited with creating the formalized mental toughness curriculum during BUD/S training, which is still used today. After his military career, he spent several years as the director of specialized performance for the Los Angeles Dodgers and contributed to the team winning three National League pennants and the 2020 World Series. He has also worked with Red Bull athletes, the US women's national soccer team, and numerous Olympic athletes, first responders, business leaders, and NASA astronauts. Eric splits his time between San Diego, California, and Whitefish, Montana, with his wife and family.

Alan Eagle is an author and executive communications coach, helping leaders and companies shape and tell their stories. He spent sixteen years at Google, partnering with executives to communicate the company's story to clients, partners, employees, and the public. He is the founder of the TDC Network, a nonprofit providing executive coaching to social impact leaders; the coauthor of the books *How Google Works* and *Trillion Dollar Coach*; and the author, all by himself, of seven letters-to-the-editor published in *Sports Illustrated*. He has never won the *New Yorker* Caption Contest. Alan lives in the San Francisco Bay Area with his wife and family.